First Corinthians

Christian Publications
3825 Hartzdale Drive, Camp Hill, PA 17011

Faithful, biblical publishing since 1883

ISBN: 0-87509-630-1
© by Christian Publications, Inc.
All rights reserved
Printed in the United States of America

96 97 98 99 00   5 4 3 2 1

#36343186

CONTENTS

Fostering Spirituality

"Spirituality" can mean many things in today's society. For the artist, it means the feelings experienced through music or painting; for the psychologist, it is that aspect of life that has to do with the inner self; for the average person, it means some dimension that is different from the five physical senses. For some, it means the practice of religion.

For believers in Jesus Christ, "spirituality" means living the "Spirit-filled life"—a life that is growing in Christlike disposition and ministry. Understood this way, spirituality can be advanced by various means at various times, depending upon the need of the individual or church—through instruction, encouragement, discipline and correction.

First Corinthians illustrates all of these methods of fostering spirituality—the Spirit-controlled life. It contains, for example, much corrective material. Like a loving father disciplining his wayward son, the Apostle Paul disciplines his erring Corinthian children, who are tolerating divisions within their assembly. He teaches them about marriage through the words of Jesus and his own Spirit-directed thought. Through his own example, he shows them how to surrender their rights for love's sake. He encourages them to exercise the gifts of the Spirit in loving ways that do not draw attention to themselves.

Whenever my father considered it necessary to punish me for willful disobedience (you can be sure it didn't happen often!), he said some things I found hard to believe at the time. "Son, this hurts me more than it hurts you!" or (this was just as hard to believe), "I'm doing this for your good." Now having experienced parenthood, I understand what my father meant and how true it was. He loved me too much to let me go undisciplined. Love always does what it knows to be best for its object. And I am thankful that my father loved me.

The writer to the Hebrews tells us in 12:6, that "the Lord disciplines those he loves, and he punishes everyone he accepts as a son." He goes on to say in verses 8-11,

> If you are not disciplined (and everyone undergoes discipline), then you are illegitimate children and not true sons. Moreover, we have all had human fathers who disciplined us and we respected them for it. How much more should we submit to the Father of our spirits and live! Our fathers disciplined us for a little while as they thought best; but God disciplines us for our good, that we may share in his holiness. No discipline seems pleasant at the time, but painful. Later on, however, it produces a harvest of righteousness and peace for those who have been trained by it.

The Church is God's family—sons and daughters of a wise and loving Father, whose purpose is to enable us to "share in His holiness." And so with infinite patience, He works with us and in us, guiding, affirming, encouraging, exhorting, pleading, enabling and, when we go astray, correcting. He sees to it that we find ourselves in the kinds of situations that crowd us to Himself. When we fail, He gently but firmly shows us where we went wrong and how to do it right—all because He loves us.

When I read First Corinthians, I am struck with how little churches and people have changed in the centuries since

Paul wrote his letter. Church policies, traditions, social customs and conventions have changed—those details in the epistle that could be called "local color." But the inner hearts, the deep desires, the human frailties and fleshly tendencies of people are still the same. We must separate out the local color and discover the abiding principles that relate to the life and conduct of local assemblies of believers in any age.

Working through First Corinthians will give a pastor opportunity to deal with truth that he might not otherwise touch in his preaching ministry. But he will never find truth that is not in some fashion applicable to the modern Church's needs.

Historical Background

The city of Corinth had been sacked and burned by the Romans in 146 B.C. Julius Caesar rebuilt it in 46 B.C., and it became the political capital of the province of Achaia. A Roman colony, the city was located in the isthmus that connected the Peloponnesus to the mainland, between the Gulf of Lechaeum on the west and the Aegean Sea on the east. Its two seaports, Lechaeum and Cenchrea, gave the city abundant trade and wealth.

The population of Corinth was cosmopolitan. Jews were there for trade, Romans were there on official business, Greeks came into the city from the country and its commerce brought people from every part of the Mediterranean world.

Dr. Merrill Tenney writes of Corinth:

Rapid growth in wealth promoted a false culture. Corinth was a "boom town" which sought luxury, display, sensuality and sport. Morally, Corinthians were regarded as inferior even according to the loose standards of paganism. They were usually represented on the Roman stage as drunk. "To live like the Corinthians" was a euphemism for the vilest kind of

life. The temple of Aphrodite in Corinth at one time
lodged one thousand priestesses who were profes-
sional prostitutes, and the ebb and flow of travel and
commerce brought to the city a floating population
that included the scum of the Mediterranean. Wealth
and dire poverty, beauty and wretchedness, culture
and squalor rubbed elbows at Corinth.[1]

Paul's Arrival in Corinth

Paul came to Corinth on his second missionary journey.
The account is told in Luke's book of Acts, beginning at
15:36. He and Silas proceeded from Antioch, north
through Syria and Cilicia, "strengthening the churches."
They revisited the believers in Lystra, Iconium and Derbe,
and went on to Troas. Here Paul received his "night vision" of the man from Macedonia begging him, "Come
over to Macedonia and help us." He and the men with
him[2] immediately set sail for the island of Samothrace,
then on to Neapolis on the east coast of Macedonia, and
then to Philippi, where they stayed for several days. Paul
and Silas were imprisoned here, and experienced the earth-
quake that released them (Acts 16). They went on from
Philippi to Thessalonica and then, after a riot, to Berea and
Athens (Acts 17).

After an unsuccessful attempt to establish a church, they
left Athens and went to Corinth, where Paul stayed for
eighteen months with fellow tentmakers Aquila and Priscilla, reasoning every Sabbath in the synagogue, trying to
persuade Jews and Greeks that Jesus was the Christ. A nega-
tive reaction in the synagogue caused Paul to transfer his
headquarters to the home of a proselyte, Titus Justus. The
ruler of the synagogue became a believer, and many of the
Corinthians believed and were baptized (Acts 18).

In company with Aquila and Priscilla, Paul left Corinth
and headed east. They stopped in Ephesus, where Aquila
and Priscilla remained and began their ministry. Eventu-

ally, Paul returned to Antioch, the church that had commissioned him. Later he returned to Ephesus where he began the longest and perhaps his most difficult ministry. Apollos, an Alexandrian Jew, also came to Ephesus and, through the ministry of Aquila and Priscilla, learned the way of God more accurately. From Ephesus, Apollos went to Corinth, where he endeared himself to many in the church.

The Writing of First Corinthians

It appears that Paul had written a previous letter to the church, which has been lost. It likely dealt with the subject of moral purity and the importance of being separated from fornicators.[3] The response of the Corinthians to this "lost letter" appears to have been unsatisfactory. Apollos had left Corinth for other fields, and the church had fallen into confusion. Chloe's slaves had brought to Paul disquieting rumors of quarreling and division in the church.

Finally, three members of the church—Stephanas, Fortunatus and Achaicus—brought a letter containing questions the Corinthians wanted clarified. In response, Paul wrote First Corinthians. It was composed near the end of his stay in Ephesus, probably in the winter of A.D. 55, during the peak of his work in that city. It was brought to Corinth by Timothy.

Endnotes

1. *New Testament Survey* (Grand Rapids, MI: William B. Eerdmans Publishing Company, 1961), 288.

2. The pronoun in Luke's account changes at 16:11 from "they" to "we," indicating possibly that at this point Luke himself joined Paul and Silas on their journey.

3. See 1 Corinthians 5:9

CHAPTER 1

Assessing the Corinthian Church

1 Corinthians 1:1-9

Paul, called to be an apostle of Christ Jesus by the will of God, and our brother Sosthenes,

To the church of God in Corinth, to those sanctified in Christ Jesus and called to be holy, together with all those everywhere who call on the name of our Lord Jesus Christ—their Lord and ours:

Grace and peace to you from God our Father and the Lord Jesus Christ.

I always thank God for you because of his grace given you in Christ Jesus. For in him you have been enriched in every way—in all your speaking and in all your knowledge—because our testimony about Christ was confirmed in you. Therefore you do not lack any spiritual gift as you eagerly wait for our Lord Jesus Christ to be revealed. He will keep you strong to the end, so that you will be blameless on the day of our Lord Jesus Christ. God, who has called you into fellowship with his Son Jesus Christ our Lord, is faithful.

I once heard the late Donald McGavran of "church growth" fame quip to a class of seminary students, "Gentlemen, if you want problems, start a church."[1] Everyone who has ever had anything to do with church life knows there is no such thing as a church without problems. Even success creates special problems.

No Pauline epistle reflects this fact more than the first letter to the church in Corinth. In his ever-so-pastoral letter, the apostle confronts theological, ethical, moral, social, spiritual and practical problems, all of which in some way or other are found in contemporary church life. From a Pauline point of view, these problems are created by the tension between life in this world's age and life in the age to come, between old man and new man behavior, between the flesh and the Spirit.

In his letter to the Galatians, Paul catalogues the works of the flesh: "sexual immorality, impurity and debauchery; idolatry and witchcraft; hatred, discord, jealousy, fits of rage, selfish ambition, dissensions, factions and envy; drunkenness, orgies, and the like" (Galatians 5:19-21). Almost all of these appear as problems in the Corinthian letter, and nearly the entire book is devoted to presenting spiritual correctives.

Notwithstanding its problems, the recipients of this letter are indeed "the *assembly of God* in Corinth." They lived in a great commercial metropolis, a New York or London of its day; a multi-racial, cross-cultural city, a city of wealth, luxury and immorality. "To live like a Corinthian" meant to live a life of debauchery. The ancient geographer Strabo called Corinth a "city of love" that attracted many because of its famous temple of Aphrodite, which contained more than a thousand priestesses of vice.[2]

Into this idolatrous and lascivious city came Saul, who became Paul, upon whom the risen Christ laid His hand on the Damascus Road, filled with the Holy Spirit and called to be an apostle (1:1), a proclaimer of the gospel to both Jew and Gentile. He found lodging with two fellow tentmakers, Aquila and Priscilla, and began to proclaim Jesus as Lord in the city's Jewish synagogue. When his message was no longer accepted by the Jews, he set up his pulpit in a house next door belonging to Titus the Just. Crispus, the synagogue ruler, his household and many of the Corinthians who heard Paul believed and were baptized.

Paul felt keenly his responsibility to accurately and faithfully proclaim the good news of Jesus. Perhaps because of the anxiety created by the physical danger the enemies of the gospel presented and the fear that he might fail in his mission in Corinth, the Lord assured him in a vision: "Do not be afraid; keep on speaking, do not be silent. For I am with you, and no one is going to attack and harm you, because I have many people in this city."[3]

The Nature of the Church (1:1-2)

Paul stayed in Corinth teaching the Word of God for a year and a half before leaving for Ephesus. During that time, and in the months following, something wonderfully new came into being in Corinth—*the assembly of God* (1:1). Popular assemblies (*ekklesia*) were part of city life in Paul's day. A herald might call the citizens to assemble for political, philosophical, oratorical, entertainment or civic purposes. But now, through the preaching of the gospel, God Himself called an assembly together in this pagan city.

It is important to understand how this assembly of God came into being. The church is here said to be "those sanctified in Christ Jesus and called to be holy" (1:2). The words "sanctify" and "holy" derive from the same Greek root, and both have the meaning of being "separated *from* the world, *unto* God for His purposes."

How does God effect this separation? It begins with the proclamation of the gospel of Jesus Christ. Paul would have begun to announce in simple, unadorned language that Jesus Christ was the Son of God, who came to earth in the flesh, died for our sins, was buried, was raised from the dead by the power of God and ascended into heaven, Lord of all. He would have called upon his hearers to repent and believe on the Lord Jesus, confessing their faith through baptism in water, and to receive by faith the Holy Spirit—the gift of the risen Christ to all who believe.

As he proclaimed this powerful message, the Holy Spirit opened the minds and hearts of divinely selected hearers, convincing them of the truth of what was being declared and of their need to repent (to change their minds) and believe the good news. They believed and were baptized, confessing Jesus Christ as Lord. In connection with their believing, the mark ("seal") of the Holy Spirit[4] was placed upon them.

This process of the Holy Spirit's awakening the hearers of the gospel—convicting them of sin, opening their hearts to believe on Jesus and to confess Him as Lord—is how God "calls" people.[5] And it is the presence of the Spirit of Christ Himself that marks believers as belonging to God, that sets them apart in Christ Jesus.

Today, when humanism reigns and individual "man is (thought to be) the measure of all things,"[6] the supernatural establishing and corporate nature of the church needs to be underscored. Believers are constituted members of the church by the gracious and powerful action of the sovereign Holy Spirit. It is God Himself who calls the church into being. We are members of *His* assembly. In these days when so much emphasis is laid upon *man's* decision for Christ, we need the balancing truth expressed in an old hymn:

> I sought the Lord, and afterward I knew
> He moved my soul to seek Him, seeking me;
> It was not I that found, O Saviour true;
> No, I was found of Thee.

> Thou didst reach forth Thy hand and mine enfold;
> I walked and sank not on the storm-vexed sea;
> 'Twas not so much that I on Thee took hold,
> As Thou, dear Lord, on me.

> I find, I walk, I love; but O the whole
> Of love is but my answer, Lord, to Thee!
> For Thou wert long beforehand with my soul;
> Always Thou lovedst me.[7]

How wonderful! Someone has beautifully reminded us that we saw God's gracious invitation written over the door, "Whosoever will may come," and we entered. As we looked back, we saw written over the inside of the door in letters of love, "Chosen in Christ before the creation of the world."

The Giftedness of the Church (1:4-7a)

In a corrective letter such as First Corinthians, Paul deems it wise to first describe what is commendable about this church. While we consider this to be a psychologically sound approach, we must not think Paul is merely saying something congenial about them in order to soften the corrective blows to come.

What Paul says about them is true. Even though much was wrong in the Corinthian assembly, they must have displayed a remarkable contrast to the heathen around them. And for this Paul gives grateful thanks.

Paul knows that reminding the church of its true state in grace, the provision that is theirs in Christ and the revelation of Jesus Christ in glory, will be a strong motivation to live in a way that is worthy of their calling.[8] Charles Spurgeon once remarked that Christians, knowing who they are in Christ and the grace of God that has abounded toward them, should be "too proud to sin"—an elegant way of saying that knowing who we really are in Christ affects our behavior.

What, then, is the true cause for thanksgiving on Paul's part when he thinks about the assembly of God in Corinth? Three great realities stand out in his mind. He is thankful for the grace, the gifts and the glory that are theirs in Christ Jesus.

All that the Corinthians possessed was not due to their own merit or excellence, but to the unmerited favor of a gracious God, who had legally and lovingly united them to Christ (1:4).[9] They had been given a rich bestowment of spiritual gifts to confirm the witness to Christ that Paul had brought to them when he proclaimed the good news (1:6). Among these many spiritual gifts graciously given were the ability to grasp the realities of the Christian faith[10] and the ability to tell others about them.[11]

The Corinthian church was no dead or dull assembly! There were no dead silences in their services, no laborious pressure to procure workers, no hollow and ritualistic approaches to worship. This church was alive in the Spirit. It had problems, yes, but correctable ones. The Corinthians needed to be taught how to exercise the gifts of the Spirit appropriately and to manifest the fruit of the Spirit (love) in their relationships. But among them was plenty of evidence of the gift-giving grace of God.

The Hope of the Church (1:7b-9)

Among them as well was a spirit of eager expectation of the revelation of Jesus Christ (1:7b). All they were enjoying of the Holy Spirit's ministry was but a deposit guaranteeing the full glory to come.[12] Paul was certain that God, who had given them the deposit, would keep them strong in their faith until the day of Christ's coming, and having credited to their account the perfect righteousness of His Son, He would present them unimpeachable (blameless) on that day.

The "age to come," ushered in by the glorious appearing of Christ, is a constant theme of Paul's letters. He recognized that his churches were already living in the age to come. But he expected to see the climax of the age in his lifetime and passed this blessed hope along to the churches he established.[13]

Dr. A.W. Tozer observed in one of his penetrating editorials[14] that the "decline of apocalyptic expectation" accounts for much of the Church's present worldliness. He believed that God's people are so comfortable that they hardly feel the need of the second coming of Christ. One wonders whether God will have to allow affliction to come to the North American Church in order to wean us from our attachment to the world.

It is still a source of great thanksgiving to us, however, as it was to Paul back then, to see the grace of God in operation in His Church today. Gifts of the Spirit are plentiful and, where administered lovingly and thoughtfully, bring great glory to the Lord who gives them.

Conclusion

The Church of Christ is a wonderfully, supernaturally conceived assembly of saints. Brought into being by the effectual working of the Holy Spirit, she is called to holiness of life—a Christlikeness made possible through a crisis infilling of the Holy Spirit, followed daily with a walk of yieldedness to the indwelling Spirit of Christ. It is vital that all members of an assembly experience this "Christ-life" in order to stand in contrast to the world in which they live.

The same Spirit who sanctifies believers also equips them for ministry through the gifts He graciously supplies. How vital that each believer be aware of the ability the Spirit has given him or her and exercise his or her gift lovingly for the good of the whole assembly. The Church need not fear the manifestations of the Spirit, which are given for the edifying of the entire assembly.

Finally, how vital it is for the believer to live this holy and useful life, waiting in expectation for the glorious appearing of our great God and Savior, Jesus Christ. John, in his first letter, tells us that "everyone who has this hope in [Christ] purifies himself, just as he is pure."[15]

Having given thanks to God for His lavish endowment of the church of God in Corinth, Paul now turns to the work of reproof and correction so greatly needed by this same church.

Endnotes

1. McGavern gave a series of church growth and mission lectures to students of Canadian Theological Seminary.

2. *The Zondervan Pictorial Bible Dictionary*, ed. Merrill C. Tenney (Grand Rapids, MI: Zondervan Publishing House, 1967), p. 183.

3. Acts 18:9-10

4. David Pawson in his book, *The Normal Christian Birth* (London: Hodder and Stoughton, 1989), pulls together New Testament history and doctrine to maintain that there are four elements in the "normal" Christian birth, *viz.*, repentance, faith, baptism in water and baptism in the Holy Spirit. Also, Dr. A.B. Simpson taught that in the book of Acts and in the initial plan of God for the New Testament church, baptism in the Spirit was intended to be part of the initiation into the Christian life. If this be so, then many of the Lord's people today are living well below the biblical norm and not experiencing all that God has for His Church.

5. While it is not within the purpose of this book to treat in detail the doctrine of "election," we note that reformed theologians speak about a general call that comes in the preaching of the gospel and about an effectual call that ensures the salvation of those whom God in His grace has chosen to give to His Son. It is this effectual call that Paul has in mind in verse 2.

6. The Sophist philosopher Protagoras who taught that there is no objective truth, only subjective, said, "Man is the measure of all things." See Frank Tilley and Ledger Wood, *A History of Philosophy* (New York: Henry Holt and Company, 1953), 57.

7. The author is anonymous; the hymn is in *Hymns* (Chicago: InterVarsity Press, 1962), number 78.

8. Paul uses this sort of motivation commonly in his letters. For example, in Ephesians 4:1 he exhorts the believers to "live a life worthy of the calling you have received." He is saying, "Behave in a manner that is in keeping with who you are in Christ." The same approach is seen in Colossians 3:1-2: "Since, then, you have been raised with Christ [their position], set your hearts on things above [behavior]."

9. The expression "in Christ" is a favorite of Paul's and rich in meaning. It speaks of a believer's identification with

Christ in His death, burial and resurrection; it speaks of the believer's union with Christ legally (justification) and experientially (sanctification). It implies that all that is true of Christ is true positionally of believers and may be appropriated by faith.

10. The Greek word is *gnosis*, meaning knowledge—in this case the knowledge of the Christian gospel and its practical consequences.

11. Greek, *logos*. There is a hint here also of those gifts of the Spirit referred to in chapter 12 that involve uttered speech, *viz.*, the word of wisdom, the word of knowledge, prophecy, tongues and the interpretation of tongues.

12. As Paul put it to the Ephesians in 1:14.

13. See, for example, First Thessalonians 1:10, where he speaks of their "wait[ing] for [God's] Son from heaven, whom he raised from the dead—Jesus, who rescues us from the coming wrath." There is both an expectation of ultimate salvation and of coming judgment, and Paul uses both aspects of the Day of the Lord to encourage and to warn the Corinthian believers.

14. A.W. Tozer, *Man: The Dwelling Place of God* (Harrisburg, PA: Christian Publications, 1966), "The Decline of Apocalyptic Expectation," 151.

15. 1 John 3:3

CHAPTER 2

Promoting Unity

1 Corinthians 1:10-31

I appeal to you, brothers, in the name of our Lord Jesus Christ, that all of you agree with one another so that there may be no divisions among you and that you may be perfectly united in mind and thought. My brothers, some from Chloe's household have informed me that there are quarrels among you. What I mean is this: One of you says, "I follow Paul"; another, "I follow Apollos"; another, "I follow Cephas"; still another, "I follow Christ."

Is Christ divided? Was Paul crucified for you? Were you baptized into the name of Paul? I am thankful that I did not baptize any of you except Crispus and Gaius, so no one can say that you were baptized into my name. (Yes, I also baptized the household of Stephanas; beyond that, I don't remember if I baptized anyone else.) For Christ did not send me to baptize, but to preach the gospel—not with words of human wisdom, lest the cross of Christ be emptied of its power.

For the message of the cross is foolishness to those who are perishing, but to us who are being saved it is the power of God. For it is written:

> *"I will destroy the wisdom of the wise;*
> *the intelligence of the intelligent I will*
> *frustrate."*

Where is the wise man? Where is the scholar? Where is the philosopher of this age? Has not God made foolish the wisdom of the world? For since in the wisdom of God the world through its wisdom did not know him, God was pleased through the foolishness of what was preached to save those who believe. Jews demand miraculous signs and Greeks look for wisdom, but we preach Christ crucified: a stumbling block to Jews and foolishness to Gentiles, but to those whom God has called, both Jews and Greeks, Christ the power of God and the wisdom of God. For the foolishness of God is wiser than man's wisdom, and the weakness of God is stronger than man's strength.

Brothers, think of what you were when you were called. Not many of you were wise by human standards; not many were influential; not many were of noble birth. But God chose the foolish things of the world to shame the wise; God chose the weak things of the world to shame the strong. He chose the lowly things of this world and the despised things—and the things that are not—to nullify the things that are, so that no one may boast before him. It is because of him that you are in Christ Jesus, who has become for us wisdom from God—that is, our righteousness, holiness and redemption. Therefore, as it is written: "Let him who boasts boast in the Lord."

Christian slaves from Chloe's household had arrived in Ephesus, likely on business for their mistress, and had reported to Paul that, among other disturbing conditions, quarrelsome divisions were creeping into the assembly of God in Corinth.

Of all the "works of the flesh" that can be manifested in a local church, nothing is more destructive of robust assembly life than a spirit of disunity. Such a spirit can show itself over the most trivial circumstances. I heard of a church in which the board could not decide where to place the garbage container in the basement. Some wanted it at one end; others at the opposite end. Eventually members of the congregation took sides with one or the other of the elder factions. It appears the real issue was not where to place the garbage container, but which side was going to win the battle for control. Division was caused over a power struggle.

In the case of the Corinthian church, the divisions arose over an unseemly exaltation of spiritual leaders. Knowing this, the apostle plunges immediately into the task of correcting this alarming and lamentable condition. His spirit is one of tender appeal, given as though the Lord Jesus Himself were exhorting the believers to be of one mind, swear allegiance to Christ alone, submit to God's wisdom and boast only in the Lord.

Being of One Mind (1:10-12)

One might imagine assorted conversations taking place in the foyer of the First Church of God in Corinth. A Gentile member asks, "Who's preaching for us next Lord's Day?" One of the elders replies, "Peter will be speaking Sunday."[1] "Oh dear," replies the Gentile member. "He'll be speaking Aramaic, and we'll need an interpreter. And he'll probably remind us that Jesus was a Jew and that the Church was born in Jerusalem and that the first believers were Jews."

Just then a Jewish believer, who happens to overhear the conversation, speaks up. "Well, what's so terrible about being Jewish? At least we weren't raised heathen like you. Peter was a Christian before Paul, and Paul just marched in and took over."

Hot words ensue, and a racist fire spreads throughout the church. "I'm for the Greek-speaking Roman citizen, Paul." "I'm for the Aramaic-speaking, day-of-Pentecost preacher, Peter."

Then that prince of intellectual preachers, that silver-tongued orator, that "mighty in the Scriptures" doctor of theology from the University of Alexandria, Apollos, speaks one Lord's day. After the service, two poorly educated slaves[2] stand together on the church steps. Says the first,

"Did you understand what he was talking about this morning?" Says the second, "Not at all. These fellows with their book-learning think they're so clever. I'll bet he'd never be able to get a job in the marketplace."

Just then one of the assembly's comparatively few university graduates walks past and overhears the conversation. "You chaps are just jealous," he remarks. "It's high time we got some educated preachers in our pulpits. I'm tired of going to church and getting so little for the mind."

"That's just your opinion," says a slave. "At least when Peter preached we could understand him. Even he couldn't always fathom Paul, and Apollos is worse. Give us Peter any day! He talks from the heart. We're for Peter."

"I'm for Apollos," replies the deep thinker.

Just then a very "spiritual" little man walks by and picks up the gist of the conversation. It had been dawning on him lately that there were really very few pure, unadulterated Christians in the church. Thank God he was one of them. He and a few others had been getting together on their own because they found it impossible to fellowship with the less spiritual members of the assembly. And this little man spits out self-righteously, "I follow Christ."

Still others in the assembly are proud they had been won to Christ by Paul, the founder of the church. They take pride in being "charter members." Despite his small stature and simplicity of speech, which some members despise, these supporters of Paul feel themselves to be in the "inner circle."

I have allowed my imagination considerable play, but I'm sure the talk in Corinth was not unlike these conversations. Mark the words Paul uses in the text and in chapter 3 to describe the situation—divisions, quarrels, jealousy. Divisive "flesh" was running uncrucified among the believers, a state of affairs that, if allowed to go on, would destroy the church.

Times have not changed. J. Stanley Glen has this pertinent comment on the Corinthian situation:

The resemblance this problem bears to that so often observed in the long history of the church at any ecclesiastical level will be fairly evident. Loyalties to those who for various reasons have acquired spiritual significance in the lives of others tend to create the kind of confidence in men that is incompatible with faith in Christ. These loyalties, of course, are not unrelated to the general category of hero worship, and in recent times to its modern equivalent, the cult of personality. . . . The name of a reformer, theologian, bishop, evangelist, teacher, or healer may easily become the object of doubtful enthusiasm. . . . Or a preacher, pastor, church official, or patron may acquire popularity and surround himself with a coterie of friends and followers, often for reasons surprisingly unrelated to the faith formally professed.[3]

God's people today must follow the apostolic exhortation, "Make every effort to keep the unity of the Spirit through the bond of peace."[4]

Allegiance to Christ (1:13-17)

Paul challenges the divisive spirit within the Corinthian assembly by asking three rhetorical questions, each of which assumes the answer, "No."

1. "Is Christ divided?"[5] If the local church is in fact the "body of Christ," then a divided body is a divided Christ—an unthinkable position. Christ is One, and the Church must demonstrate this oneness.

2. "Was Paul crucified for you?" By focusing their loyalties on Paul, they were putting him in the place of the One who was crucified for their sins, making Paul their savior. Certainly Paul had placed his life on the line for lost men; he had more than once been thought dead. But Paul knew that Christ's death on the cross had a significance far beyond any death he might have died. That

Paul was crucified for them was unthinkable. However exemplary an apostolic martyrdom would be, only Christ's death was substitutionary.

3. "Were you baptized into the name of Paul?" Had the Corinthians recognized the meaning of their baptism, they would know they had been baptized into Christ, not into any man. Their identification was not with Paul, but with the death, burial and resurrection of the Lord Jesus.

Leon Morris, quoting Robertson and Plummer, observes that

> " 'into the name' implies entrance into fellowship and allegiance, such as exists between the Redeemer and the redeemed." There could be no suggestion that Paul had said or done anything to bring his converts into such a relation to him personally. He had pointed men to Christ.[6]

Realizing how the Corinthians could distort the implications of their baptism, Paul reminds them that he had baptized very few of them, since his calling was not to do the work of a church elder, but to proclaim the "word of the cross" (1:14–17).[7] With this, Paul begins to strike at the heart of the Corinthian divisions. If they had really understood the cross, they would not have exalted men.

Submission to God's Wisdom (1:18-25)

In this portion of the text, the apostle contrasts what he calls "the wisdom of man" with "the wisdom of God." Evidently within the Corinthian assembly some were in danger of putting inordinate emphasis on "wisdom" as it was understood by the world of that day. Paul knew that worldly wisdom was the driving force behind the development of divisions. Hence he must warn the church about allowing the spirit of the age to encroach upon the thinking of God's people.

He begins (1:18a) by observing that the message[8] of the cross is utter nonsense to the worldly wise. To proclaim that the man Jesus was none other than God incarnate, that He died for our sins, was buried, rose and was seen by selected witnesses, and that salvation is through Him to all who believe,[9] made no more sense to the intelligentsia of Paul's day than it makes sense to the worldly thinkers of our generation.

Ultimately, says Paul, a person's response to the message of the cross determines one's destiny. To reject the cross puts one on the road to eternal death; to embrace the cross, wherein one sees the power of God, results in eternal salvation (1:18b).

The wisdom of the wisest philosopher, the scholarship of the most scholarly doctor of theology, the natural intelligence of the most intelligent debater cannot bring one to the knowledge of God. God not only disregards all humanly devised attempts to know Him, He counts them as foolishness. In contrast, God has ordained that through the message that worldly-minded men call foolishness, all who believe truly come to know God and become the partakers of eternal salvation (1:19–21).[10]

In verses 22 and 23, Paul makes clear why the message of a crucified Savior is such foolishness to both the unbelieving Jew and Greek. For the Jews, the thought of a crucified Messiah was a "stumbling block" for two reasons.

First, they expected their Messiah to perform certain signs. Even while Paul was writing, many self-confessed Messiahs were appealing to Jews, beguiling them with the promise of miraculous signs.

For example, in A.D. 45, a man called Theudas persuaded thousands of Jews to follow him to the Jordan River by promising that the water would divide at his command and he would lead them across. In A.D. 54, a man from Egypt claimed to be a prophet and persuaded 30,000 people to follow him by promising that at his word the walls of Jerusalem would fall down.[11]

Jesus Himself resisted the devil's temptation to work a sign by throwing Himself from the temple wall to get a following.

Jewish tradition said the Messiah would repeat Moses' miracle of bringing down manna from heaven. Hence the Jews suggested that Jesus prove His Messiahship by doing this again.[12] When Jesus cleansed the temple of money changers, the Jews demanded He produce a miraculous sign to prove His authority. Jesus replied with the astounding words, "Destroy this temple, and I will raise it again in three days," referring to His death and resurrection.[13]

Second, it was incredible to the Jews that one whose life ended on a cross could possibly be God's Anointed. Didn't the Scripture say, "Anyone who is hung on a tree is under God's curse?"[14] Therefore, the cross proved that Jesus was not the Christ.

For the Greeks, preaching about the cross was foolishness because they "look[ed] for wisdom" (1:22b). Barclay tells us that for them wisdom meant a man with "a clever mind and a cunning tongue, a mental acrobat, a man who with glittering and persuasive rhetoric could make the worse appear the better reason." He quotes Chrysostom describing the wise men: "They croak like frogs in a marsh; they are the most wretched of men, because, though ignorant, they think themselves wise; they are like peacocks, showing off their reputation and the number of their pupils as peacocks do their tails."[15]

Furthermore, the concepts of sin, guilt and atonement were repugnant to Greek philosophy, negating the need for the cross. So when a blunt little fellow without oratorical skills comes into their city proclaiming a God come in the flesh, who was crucified for their sins and raised from the dead, they scornfully laugh at him. Utter idiocy! And yet for those among them whose hearts God opened to believe the gospel, this Jesus Christ is seen to be the wisdom and power of God, wiser than man's wisdom, stronger than man's strength (1:24-25).

Boasting Only in the Lord (1:26-31)

Paul concludes his argument by reminding the Corinthians of the sorts of people that compose their assembly. For the most part they are not the intellectuals or the prestigious or the nobility of Corinth. Perhaps Aquila and Priscilla, Gaius, Crispus and Erastus—the city treasurer—might fit into those categories, but the greater balance of the congregation would be catalogued as uneducated, weak nobodies in the eyes of upper-crust Corinth. There is no point in any of them trying to think otherwise.

This is not because things just happened to turn out that way. What we have here is God's deliberately working out His divine purposes through calling people whom the world's thinkers would consider unsuitable. What an illustration is the Corinthian church of the truth of God's Word through the prophet: " 'For my thoughts are not your thoughts, neither are your ways my ways,' declares the LORD. 'As the heavens are higher than the earth, so are my ways higher than your ways and my thoughts than your thoughts.' "[16]

Only God would have thought of doing it this way. The wisdom of a crucified Savior, of a divine strategy that has united believers to the Christ and made Him become for them true wisdom, righteousness, holiness and redemption. How could anyone understanding the word of the cross possibly glory in Paul or Apollos or Peter? Rather, "Let him who boasts boast in the Lord" (1:30–31).

Conclusion

Two thousand years have passed since Paul wrote to the church in Corinth. Yet all that he wrote is powerfully applicable to the Church today. The text calls us to hear the voice of the Holy Spirit warning us to be on guard against the devil's sowing seeds of division among God's people. If he succeeds in stirring up such a destructive spirit, he brings the reputation of the Church and of its Lord into disrepute.

Paul's words to his son in the faith, Titus, are as appropriate in today's Church as ever: "Warn a divisive person once, and then warn him a second time. After that, have nothing to do with him. You may be sure that such a man is warped and sinful; he is self-condemned."[17]

We, like the Corinthians, need to ask ourselves if we are in danger of glorying in man instead of in Christ. Is denominational pride creeping into our collective spirit—a pride that cuts us off from fellowship with believers of a different persuasion? Do our attitudes say, "I am of Simpson"; "I am of Wesley"; "I am of Luther"; "I am of Calvin"; or "I am non-denominational"? Such attitudes grieve the Holy Spirit, the Lord of the Church, and stifle His work among us.

Our passage also teaches that man's worldly wisdom succeeds only in driving him far from the knowledge of God. Let us never be guilty of relying on worldly wisdom. Let us, rather, remember that it is only the Word of the cross that is "the power of God for the salvation of everyone who believes: first for the Jew, then for the Gentile."[18] And let us, with Paul, never be ashamed of this gospel. It is the only message that has power to transform lives and deliver from eternal death. If you have not yet trusted in Christ alone, do so without delay.

Endnotes

1. Actually we have no evidence that Peter ever visited Corinth.

2. We are not to understand that all slaves of Paul's day were illiterate or uneducated.

3. *Pastoral Problems in First Corinthians* (Philadelphia, PA: The Westminster Press, 1964), 16.

4. Ephesians 4:3

5. There is some possibility that the Greek could be translated as an exclamatory statement, "Christ stands divided!" but the context seems to favor the question.

6. *The First Epistle of Paul to the Corinthians* (London: The Tyndale Press, 1958), 42.

7. He does not say why he baptized Crispus and Gaius and the household of Stephanus, but it cannot have been because of their importance in the community. For helpful insight into this passage, see Graydon F. Snyder, *First Corinthians, a Faith Community* (Macon, GA: Mercer University Press, 1992), 17.

8. Literally "the word of the cross."

9. This, according to First Corinthians 15:1-4, was precisely the message that Paul had proclaimed in Corinth.

10. The King James rendering of verse 21—"the foolishness of preaching"—is misleading, as though the act of preaching itself were foolish. The Greek word, translated "preaching" is *kerugma*, which refers not to the method, but to the content of what is preached. For examples of the *kerugma* of the apostolic preachers, the reader should study the sermons recorded in the book of Acts.

11. Cited by William Barclay, *The Letters to the Corinthians* (Philadelphia, PA: The Westminster Press, 1977), 19.

12. John 6:30-31

13. John 2:19

14. Deuteronomy 21:23

15. *Letters*, 19.

16. Isaiah 55:8-9

17. Titus 3:10-11

18. Romans 1:16

CHAPTER 3

Attaining to the Wisdom of God

1 Corinthians 2

When I came to you, brothers, I did not come with eloquence or superior wisdom as I proclaimed to you the testimony about God. For I resolved to know nothing while I was with you except Jesus Christ and him crucified. I came to you in weakness and fear, and with much trembling. My message and my preaching were not with wise and persuasive words, but with a demonstration of the Spirit's power, so that your faith might not rest on men's wisdom, but on God's power.

We do, however, speak a message of wisdom among the mature, but not the wisdom of this age or of the rulers of this age, who are coming to nothing. No, we speak of God's secret wisdom, a wisdom that has been hidden and that God destined for our glory before time began. None of the rulers of this age understood it, for if they had, they would not have crucified the Lord of glory. However, as it is written:

> *"No eye has seen,*
> *no ear has heard,*
> *no mind has conceived*
> *what God has prepared for those who love*
> *him"—*
> *but God has revealed it to us by his Spirit.*

The Spirit searches all things, even the deep things of God. For who among men knows the thoughts of a man except the man's spirit within him? In the same way no one knows the thoughts of God except the Spirit of God. We have not received the spirit of the world but the Spirit who is from God, that we may understand what God has freely given us. This is what we speak, not in words taught us by human wisdom but in words taught by the Spirit, expressing spiritual truths in spiritual words. The man without the Spirit does not accept the things that come from the Spirit of God, for they are foolishness to him, and he cannot understand them, because they are spiritually discerned. The spiritual man makes judgments about all things, but he himself is not subject to any man's judgment:

> *"For who has known the mind of the Lord*
> *that he may instruct him?"*

But we have the mind of Christ.

I recall being invited to address a noon-hour evangelistic effort sponsored by Christians on the campus of a prominent university. This would necessitate, I immediately thought, an intellectual approach to my presentation of the gospel, so I prepared a profound and polished discourse calculated to persuade my educated hearers of the truth of the gospel message.

But as the address progressed, my mouth began to get dry. I noticed the students were not listening with interest, and I began to panic. Then I observed my pastor friend sitting on the front row with his head bowed in prayer.

Suddenly the thought occurred to me: "Just present the gospel simply, as you would to any man on the street. Stop trying to impress them with your scholarly polish." I set aside my prepared lecture and proclaimed Christ crucified, buried and risen, in terms that a child could understand.

The students began to listen, and I learned a lesson I hope I never forget.

The Simplicity of God's Wisdom (2:1-5)

Some think that when Paul preached to the Athenians on Mars Hill,[1] he fell prey to the same temptation by attempting to reduce the Christian message to philosophical terms. One expositor suggests this might well have been the reason why in Athens he had one of his very few failures. He suggests:

> It would almost seem that he had said to himself, "Never again! From henceforth I will tell the story of Jesus in utter simplicity. I will never again try to wrap it up in human categories. I will know nothing but Jesus Christ, and Him upon His Cross."[2]

Whether or not his observation is correct, it is clear that by the time Paul arrived in Corinth from Athens, the manner and content of his proclamation had been fixed.

Notice first Paul's manner (2:1, 3-4). He did not try to demonstrate the superior oratorical ability that would have given him status among the worldly-wise Corinthians. He had already made it clear in 1:17 that this would empty the cross of its power. Such a display of eloquence would distract his hearers from the content of the message and focus their attention on the preacher's mastery of language. The message would have no real or lasting effect on their lives.

Instead he tells the Corinthians the real feelings he experienced as he undertook his mission among them. Notice the words he uses: "weakness," "fear," "trembling." He is not likely describing physical weakness, but rather a sense of his utter helplessness, his inability to persuade his hearers to believe. The fear he feels is not so much for his life or safety, though that may well be there, as it is fear that he will fail in the mission to which he has been called. The trembling is not an outward display of nervousness, but an inward quaking of soul in the face of the task before him.

Any preacher who stands before a congregation with the Word of God in his hand can identify with Paul. He will know that unless the anointing of the Holy Spirit is upon him, giving what the old divines called "unction," he may as well not preach. I am reminded of the story of the Scottish minister who failed to show up in his pulpit when the service was to begin. An elder went to the study to summon the pastor and heard him repeating over and over to an unseen Presence, "Except You go with me, I will not go up."[3]

A congregation may be listening to a preacher who is well prepared, who has honestly and accurately done his exegetical, hermeneutical and homiletical work. What they may not see is the inner turmoil he is experiencing as he speaks, lest his preparation not have included the preparedness of spirit that causes the Word to bring to the people's hearts the effect they need.

Notice second Paul's message (2:1-2). He calls it "the testimony about God" (literally "of God"). This does not mean Paul's personal testimony of what God has done for him, or what God means to him. Rather it is the passing on of the message that God has given about Himself and His Son. The gospel Paul preaches is not of his own making, but has been given to him by God Himself.[4]

The content of his proclamation is "Jesus Christ and him crucified" (2:2, literally, "this one crucified"). Paul could have brought to the Corinthians many truths concerning Jesus Christ, but these would have to wait till later. He could have conveyed many teachings that came from the lips of Jesus. But to bring the teachings of Christ before the preaching of the cross of Christ could have resulted in their seeing the gospel as another set of moral principles.

The first message the Corinthians must hear is a proclamation of One who died for their sins, bearing their transgressions in His own body on the cross, freeing them from guilt by His death that made atonement for sin. This was the life-changing message they needed to receive and believe.

Notice third the confirmation of Paul's message (2:4-5). What convinced the Corinthians of the truth of the gospel was not "wise and persuasive words," but the "demonstration[5] of the Spirit's power." Paul is not just referring to the Spirit's power to change people's lives or the power that was upon him as he preached. He is referring to the signs that accompanied the preaching of the gospel.

The Lord Jesus had promised that such signs would take place,[6] and the writer to the Hebrews avows that "God also testified to [the truth of the gospel] by signs, wonders and various miracles, and gifts of the Holy Spirit distributed according to his will."[7] No doubt Paul has in mind as well the varied manifestations of the Spirit to which he refers in chapter 12. These visible demonstrations of the Spirit's power would confirm to the Corinthians the truth of the gospel message, where mere wise words would not. Their faith would thus rest upon the manifest power of God.

I find it thrilling to know that God still bears witness to the truth of the gospel today as He did in the apostolic age, by signs and wonders. My heart is filled with holy excitement when I hear reports from missionaries who tell of the miracles of healing experienced, not just by the Christians, but by unbelieving hearers of the Word of Christ as well in such areas as South America or Southeast Asia.

One report comes from a preacher in Africa where, during an evangelistic service, widespread healings of crippled limbs, blind eyes and deaf ears were confirmed.[8] These sovereign displays of God's power attest to the truth of the gospel that is being preached, and thousands believe in Christ as a result. We can be thankful to God whenever the same phenomena accompany the preaching of the gospel in North America, as they often do in those areas where the Holy Spirit is reviving Christ's Church.

The Hiddenness of God's Wisdom (2:6-9)

Paul has been showing his readers the inability of human wisdom to come to the knowledge of God. He has reminded them that in his own proclamation of the gospel he avoided the methods of the philosophers and orators of his day that drew attention to their own skillful ability to persuade. Thus far he has used the word "wisdom" in a bad sense to mean the "skilled marshaling of human arguments, employed with a view to convincing the hearer" or truth evaluated in terms of human standards rather than those given in Christ crucified.[9]

We must not think, however, that the Christian gospel is foolish or unwise. That which the world considers foolishness is really the most profound wisdom. And Paul now describes this divine wisdom in verses 6–9.

The "message of wisdom" of which he speaks is nothing other than the word of the cross (1:18)—a message that can be understood only by the "mature," who, according to Calvin, are those who "possess a sound and unbiased judgment (2:6a)."[10] It is not "the wisdom of this age," which finds its roots in man's rebellion against God.[11] Nor is it the wisdom of the "rulers of this age" (2:6b)—the politicians, the educators, the intellectuals, the unbelieving philosophers whom the world holds in such high esteem because of their position but who will nevertheless all perish in the end.

The modern mass media is today's devoted communicator of the widsom of the age. The existence of a personal God is implicitly (and often explicitly) denied, and Christians are portrayed as mindless idiots whose goal is to foist their outdated beliefs on society in general. All morality is relative. The idea of sin is outdated and personal salvation, therefore, unnecessary. Science is god. The theory of evolution accounts for humanity's existence, and creationism is not worthy of intelligent discussion because a human is just another animal. The only salvation humans need is rescue from oppressive social structures which enslave them in ignorance and poverty. Happiness, purchased by money, is the goal for which they strive, and education is the savior that ensures that they will reach their goal.

Malcolm Muggeridge vividly describes his conclusions about this world's wisdom:

Education, the great mumbo-jumbo and fraud of this age, purports to equip us to live, and is prescribed as a universal remedy for everything from juvenile delinquency to premature senility. For the most part, it only serves to enlarge stupidity, inflate conceit, enhance credulity and put those subjected to it at the mercy of brainwashers with printing presses, radio and television at their disposal. I have seen pictures of huge, ungainly, prehistoric monsters who developed such a weight of protective shell that they sank under its burden and became extinct. Our civilization likewise is sinking under the burden of its own wealth, and the necessity to consume it; of its own happiness, and the necessity to provide and sustain the fantasies which embody it; of its own security, and the ever more fabulously destructive nuclear devices considered essential to it.[12]

The wisdom of this age is utterly contrary to God's revealed wisdom. The wisdom of God consists of a plan of salvation through a crucified Saviour, a wisdom that was in the heart of God from before the creation of the world, that will ultimately insure the glorification of all who believe (2:7), but that is not accepted by a man without the Spirit (2:14).[13]

The Revealer of God's Wisdom (2:10-16)

In contrast to the ignorance of the rulers of this age who, without the Holy Spirit, cannot "[conceive] . . . what God has prepared for those who love him" (2:9),[14] we who have received the Spirit are able to grasp God's revelation (2:10). The Holy Spirit Himself is the able revealer of the things of God, because there is absolutely nothing in God's mind which the Holy Spirit cannot fathom and reveal. Just as the self-consciousness of a man knows his own thoughts like no one else, so the Spirit of God alone knows the thoughts of God (2:11). Therefore those who possess the

Holy Spirit are capable, through His enabling, of understanding the blessings that are freely given them by God's grace (2:12).

What a powerful portion of Scripture! It teaches us that not only did the Holy Spirit inspire the authors of Scripture to write what they did, but it is He who illuminates the minds of believers so that we can comprehend and receive the gospel that is recorded. He is the only Agent of revelation, inspiration and illumination.

I remember once viewing missionary slides from the Baliem Valley, and thinking, *How could those poor heathen possibly comprehend the message that the missionaries are bringing to them?* But the truth is that the most educated, scholarly, brilliant North American churchman cannot grasp the truth of God any better than his Baliem Valley kinsman. Both are utterly dependent upon the Holy Spirit's opening their understanding.

How appropriate, then, is Andrew Reed's hymn verse:

> Holy Ghost, with light divine,
> Shine upon this heart of mine:
> Chase the shades of night away;
> Turn my darkness into day.

Conclusion

Our text sets before us a truth that cannot be emphasized enough at this time in Church history. In an age when modern technology, pastoral psychology, oratorical expertise and inventive pedagogical methodologies can all bring apparent "success" to our religious endeavors, we tend to forget or ignore how dependent we are upon the Holy Spirit to bring understanding of spiritual truth to the human mind.

Like Samson who, when he tried to take on the Philistines, "did not know that the LORD had left him"[15] and so was defeated, we busy twentieth-century Christians may mistake our apparent successes for the work of the Holy

Spirit and discover all too late that we have been ministering in the energy of the flesh.

Let us be sure that we have the anointing of the Holy Spirit upon us. Someone has well said, "God does not anoint techniques or methods, but people." The kinds of ministry challenges that the Church faces today require nothing less than Spirit-anointed servants. How else can we begin to touch the confused, dysfunctional, broken, helpless people of the world with the healing, life-giving message of the gospel. They need to see the power of God manifested through His people.

Endnotes

1. Acts 17:16ff

2. William Barclay, *Letters to the Corinthians*, 23.

3. Reflecting the words of Moses to the Lord in Exodus 33:15; see also Exodus 4:10; Isaiah 6:5; and Jeremiah 1:6 for similar attitudes in God's servants.

4. See Galatians 1:11-12

5. The word is *apodeixis*, which means literally "proof "— the most rigorous kind of proof.

6. See Mark 16:17, the manuscript problem notwithstanding!

7. Hebrews 2:4

8. Reported by a German evangelist on "The 700 Club."

9. C.K. Barrett, *A Commentary on the First Epistle to the Corinthians* (London: A & C Black, 1968), 67.

10. John Calvin, *Commentary on the Epistles of Paul the Apostle to the Corinthians*, Vol. 1 (Edinburgh: The Calvin Translation Society, 1848), 102.

11. Barret, 70.

12. Malcolm Muggeridge, *Jesus Rediscovered*, (London: Collins Sons & Company, 1969), 53.

13. The word translated "accept" (*dechomai*), can also be translated, "put up with" or "tolerate." (Arndt and Ging-

rich, 176). This would imply that not only does the man without the Spirit not understand the things of God, but that he is expressly hostile to them. Compare Romans 8:7, "the sinful mind is hostile to God."

14. The passage in Isaiah 64:4 reads "no one has heard, no ear has perceived, no eye has seen any God besides you, who acts on behalf of those who *wait* for him" (emphasis added). It appears as though either Paul's memory failed him at this point or (and likely), under the inspiration of the Holy Spirit, he interpreted the passage freely to suit his purposes. Calvin, p. 107, observes that "waiting for God is the certain product and effect of love to him."

15. Judges 16:20

CHAPTER 4

Seeing Ministers Through God's Eyes

1 Corinthians 3

Brothers, I could not address you as spiritual but as worldly—mere infants in Christ. I gave you milk, not solid food, for you were not yet ready for it. Indeed, you are still not ready. You are still worldly. For since there is jealousy and quarreling among you, are you not worldly? Are you not acting like mere men? For when one says, "I follow Paul," and another, "I follow Apollos," are you not mere men?

What, after all, is Apollos? And what is Paul? Only servants, through whom you came to believe—as the Lord has assigned to each his task. I planted the seed, Apollos watered it, but God made it grow. So neither he who plants, nor he who waters is anything, but only God, who makes things grow. The man who plants and the man who waters have one purpose, and each will be rewarded according to his own labor. For we are God's fellow workers; you are God's field, God's building.

By the grace God has given me, I laid a foundation as an expert builder, and someone else is building on it. But each one should be careful how he builds. For no one can lay any foundation other than the one already laid, which is Jesus Christ. If any man builds on this foundation using gold, silver, costly stones, wood, hay or straw, his work will be shown for what it is, because the Day will bring it to light. It will be revealed with fire, and the fire will test the quality of each man's work. If what he has built survives, he will receive his reward. If it is burned up, he will suffer loss; he himself will be saved, but only as one escaping through the flames.

Don't you know that you yourselves are God's temple and that God's Spirit lives in you? If anyone destroys God's temple, God will destroy him; for God's temple is sacred, and you are that temple.

Do not deceive yourselves. If any one of you thinks he is wise by the standards of this age, he should become a "fool" so that he may become wise. For the wisdom of this world is foolishness in God's sight. As it is written: "He catches the wise in their craftiness"; and again, "The Lord knows that the thoughts of the wise are futile." So then, no more boasting about men! All things are yours, whether Paul or Apollos or Cephas or the world or life or death or the present or the future—all are yours, and you are of Christ, and Christ is of God.

The other afternoon, my wife and I went for a long drive into the country to enjoy the beauty of God's creation. The corn was tall in the fields, and as we drove by one of those luscious expanses, we thought we heard loud talking, so we pulled over to the side of the road to listen. You will have to take our word for it; and if you have any kind of an imagination, you won't find it unbelievable if we tell you that the conversation we heard was coming from the corn stalks!

One stalk, who seemed to be the spokesperson for several rows, called over to another, "Who planted the kernels you came from?" A second stalk called back, "Farmer Paulson, the most successful farmer in the area!" First stalk: "I'm sorry for you; you should have been planted by Farmer Lopston, as we were. He has a unique way of sowing the seed." Second stalk: "That's nothing. Farmer Paulson, who planted us, sticks to the old ways of planting and obviously gets better results."

Just then a third stalk spoke up, and we heard him say, "The secret of our phenomenal growth in our section of the field is Farmer Peterson's modern irrigation system. Who watered you?"

Second stalk: "Farmer Timson watered us; he uses special hoses that drive the water in much deeper than Peterson's system."

Just then we heard a Jersey cow in the pasture next to the corn speak up. He had apparently been listening to the dialogue: "Your thinking is all wrong, fellows. Everybody knows it's neither the sower nor the irrigator that accounts for your lovely growth. It's the power in the seed that counts." After that the voices just seemed to fade away, and we drove on.

The Corinthian believers, like the stalks in the field, were boasting about their planters and waterers, failing to see that it was God who made things grow. Paul had to show them what lay at the bottom of their leader-oriented divisions. In chapters 1 and 2, he had made clear they were being influenced by the worldly-wise spirit of the Corinthian culture. Instead of the church influencing the city, the spirit of the city was influencing the church. But something inside the Corinthian Christians themselves gave ground to this spirit, and Paul tells them pointedly what that was.

They Are Not to Be Idolized (3:1-4)

The Corinthians had a fleshly view of their spiritual leaders. They were allowing their fallen, animal instincts and appetites (the flesh) to control their behavior.[1] When they first heard and believed the gospel as "infants in Christ," they were not aware of the power of the flesh. Although it influenced their attitudes, they were not willfully yielding to its power. Paul had only to minister to them as immature believers, "not yet ready for [solid food]" (3:2).

But now, even after more thorough instruction by both Paul and Apollos, they are still not ready for solid food. They are still worldly (3:3), allowing the flesh to work actively as a ruling principle within them,[2] manifesting itself in "jealousy and quarreling." Rather than behaving like new men in Christ, men possessing the Spirit, they are behaving like ordinary men without the Spirit.

The spiritual life has three great enemies: the world, the flesh and the devil. The devil, Satan, that sworn enemy of God and the saints, tempts believers to sin through (1) the allurement of the world system that is under his temporary control and (2) the flesh, those animal instincts and appetites that pervade fallen human nature. Before faith in Christ and baptism in the Spirit, the "works of the flesh" controlled our lives to a greater or lesser degree.[3]

But now thanks to the indwelling of the Holy Spirit, a stronger power is within us so that we need not be in bondage any longer to the flesh. It is necessary, however, for us to yield ourselves to the Spirit, since the one to whom we yield is the one who has control.[4] Thank God it is true that as a matter of usual practice, spiritual people yield to the Spirit and do not "fulfill the desires of the flesh."

But at this point in their Christian lives the Corinthians were too easily yielding to the flesh, manifested in their jealous and quarrelsome divisions around their spiritual leaders. Paul will now lead them into spiritual rather than fleshly thinking about himself and Apollos.

They Are God's Servants (3:5-9)

This passage has three arguments or lines of thought, each calculated to give the Corinthian church a right view of the godly leaders whom they are exalting.

The first is the Relative Insignificance of Farmhands (3:6-7). Paul uses an agricultural analogy in which he likens the church to a field of grain (3:9).

Someone has to plant the seed first. Paul had done this when he came to Corinth and proclaimed the seed of the

Word of the gospel. Someone then has to water the seed. This was the work of Apollos and other teachers in ministry to the newly formed church. But the work of planting and watering is fruitless unless some force in nature causes growth. And when it came to the existence of a church in Corinth, only God could bring that into being.

How foolish it is for the church to boast about who planted them or who watered them—dividing over "farm hands." Paul is saying, "The identity of the farmer is not as important as you are making it. Don't boast in your farmer; boast in God, who put life in the seed and causes you to grow up into Christ."

It is appropriate, of course, for believers to appreciate the evangelist who first brought the gospel to them. It is fitting to give a special place in your heart to the pastor who fed you with the milk and meat of the Word of God. But it is improper to make little gods out of these who cannot produce the church. The men and women Christ uses in His field are not as important as the Christ who uses them, and the God who, in His mercy and by a miracle of divine grace, brings a church into being. Paul is saying, "Let's get our perspectives straight. God will not give His glory to men. To Him alone belongs all the honor."

I read about a young preacher (the story may be apocryphal) who, unlike Paul, was becoming increasingly aware of his own great importance to the kingdom of God. It began to dawn on him that he was quite indispensable to God, and he did not know what would happen to his church if he were to be suddenly taken from them.

His bishop, recognizing what was happening, called him into his office and placed a bowl of water on the desk. He instructed the young preacher to place his finger in the water and then remove it. When the young fellow had done as he was told, the bishop announced, "Young man, the size of the hole that is left in the water is comparable to your relative importance in the kingdom of God!"

Perhaps some of us preachers need to keep a bowl of

water on our desks to stick our fingers into from time to time
to remind us that we are only farmhands!

A second argument that Paul presents to convince the
Corinthians not to divide around their preachers could be
called the Argument from Assigned Labor (3:5). He calls
Apollos and himself "servants . . . as the Lord has assigned to
each his task." The word used for "servants" (*diakonoi*) is the
word from which we get our English word "deacon." Its
original meaning was a "table waiter," and it came to be used
for the servant of a master.[5] It stresses the lowly character of
the service rendered.[6] The Corinthians needed to be reminded that these men whom they were setting up as their
heroes were really God's errand boys whom He raised up
for their good.

Furthermore, they were men who did not choose their
own tasks as servants (3:5b). Paul didn't say, "I think I'd like
to be a missionary and plant churches. That's a good career
and more important than pastoring a church." Apollos didn't
announce, "I think I'll go to seminary in Alexandria and
learn to be a great expositor of the Scriptures. There will be
considerable prestige attached to this ministry." Paul was a
planter and Apollos a waterer because the Lord laid hold of
their lives, sovereignly gifting them as He chose and sending
them off on His errands to do His will. They were just doing what they had been told.

The Corinthians must not boast about the errand boys.
Rather they ought to boast in the Lord, the Head of the
Church, who assigned the ministers to their respective ap-
pointments and gifted them to do their individual work.

A third argument Paul uses is the Argument from a Unified Purpose (3:8-9a). The planter and the waterer, the culti-
vator and the weeder, are all on the same team. They are not
in competition. What they each desire is the glory of God
and a healthy, unified, growing, maturing church. Each has
his part to play, but the goal is one. It is God's goal, and Paul
and Apollos are working together with Him to reach the
goal.

The coach of a team sport does not try to produce individual stars, each doing his own thing. He wants a squad of players who will surrender their individualism and learn to work together as a team to reach the goal of winning the game. The Corinthian church needed to get hold of the truth that their Christian leaders were not individualists seeking stardom, but a team seeking corporate victory.

Their Work Will Be Appraised (3:10-17)

Paul now changes the metaphor from agriculture to architecture. He likens the church to a building, himself to an expert contractor who has laid a firm substructure and others who followed him as building a superstructure upon the foundation he laid (3:10). The builders must avoid two mistakes. They must not seek to build another foundation than the one that has been laid, and they must take great care to erect an edifice worthy of the foundation on which they are building, one that will pass close inspection.

The analogy is clear. The foundation that Paul has laid is Christ Himself. He had been commissioned by the grace of God to travel the Roman world, laying foundations in every city through the preaching of the gospel. It seems that apart from one or two exceptions, he stayed in one place long enough to lay the groundwork, and then moved on, letting others do the building through pastoral teaching.

His concern is that those who do the pastoral work should do it adequately, in a manner worthy of Christ, the foundation. They have a choice of materials to use—valuable and imperishable, or worthless and perishable. They must continually remember that the true nature of their labor will be revealed on that Day when the Lord will judge the quality of each man's work.

Having made clear the significance and nature of his own and Apollos' work, and having made sure the Corinthians understand the weighty responsibility their leaders have to them and to God, Paul now identifies the building and sends a clear warning to those who would perpetrate divisions in the church.

The building is a holy temple,[7] not made with hands out of brick and mortar, but the Corinthian church itself (3:16). They corporately are the dwelling place of the Spirit of God. As the temple in the Old Testament was to be a thing of beauty and glory, reflecting the nature of Israel's God, so the New Testament temple (the Church) is created to bring honor and glory to our God and His Christ—a place set apart for His exclusive use (sacred).

What a treacherous deed it would be, therefore, to destroy the temple of the living God—so terrible that God Himself would destroy the destroyer (3:17). Yet this is exactly what the divisiveness in Corinth was in danger of doing, and the people guilty of this blasphemy were leaving themselves open to death. Paul's word here comes as the most powerful warning yet against the fleshly divisiveness that was tearing the church apart.

They Are All for the Church's Good (3:18-23)

Chapter 3 concludes with a reminder to the church of the folly of "boasting about men." God has wisely given Paul, Apollos and Peter as gifts to the church. All three belong to the people of God, so why should any member rob himself by claiming to belong to just one of them (3:21)?

Finally, in a beautiful lyric style that takes him far beyond the problem in Corinth, Paul ascribes to the church the possession of all things present or future. The world is ours inasmuch as ultimately we will reign over it with Christ. Life is ours inasmuch as we are united to Christ, who is the Life. Death is ours since through Christ's resurrection we too have conquered it. The present and the future are ours, filled with victory as we live in the power of Christ Himself.

But that is not all! We belong to Christ (3:23). He has purchased us with His own atoning blood; He is our Lord and Master, and we are united to Him by the Spirit. And Christ belongs to God. To procure everything that is in our inheritance as the people of God, the Son submitted Himself to the will of the Father and became obedient unto the death of the cross. As a reward for His sufferings, God put all things under His lordship,[8] in order that ultimately the Son might put all things, including Himself, under subjection to the Father, that God may be all in all.[9]

Conclusion

Three important lessons are displayed in our passage. First, it is important to recognize and deal ruthlessly with "the flesh." Just how mercilessly we should deal with it is made clear by both Paul and our Lord. The apostle tells us to "put to death the deeds of the flesh."[10] And Jesus, in His Sermon on the Mount tells us to "gouge out" or "cut off" offending body parts.[11]

What a terrible thing it is to allow uncrucified flesh to cause the breakup of a local church of Christ! Whether through heresies or (more likely) insistence on having one's own way, the exaltation of human leadership, the irresponsibility of that leadership or through any other means, the name of Christ is slandered and God's glory spoiled. We must resist any temptation to tolerate such behavior in ourselves and in our assemblies.

Second, our text teaches us the enormous importance of doing valuable and imperishable work as God's servants. What sort of work is valuable and imperishable, and what is worthless and perishable? Generally the former is whatever is done in the power and direction of the Spirit, while the latter is what is done in the strength of the flesh.

What sort of pastoral work does the Spirit delight to empower? Perhaps most importantly, careful, prayerful, well-studied exposition of Scripture. The teaching pastor's work is to let the Word of God speak for itself as he searches out the meaning of its words and phrases and the context in which they appear and applies them wisely to the life situations in which his people find themselves. A wise pastor will resist the temptation to try to do everything that everyone thinks he ought to be doing, and thus fail in the most important thing.[12] And a wise congregation will seek to place itself under the ministry of a Bible-teaching pastor, appointing others to do the work of administration and planning.

Third, the passage encourages God's people to value the variety of ministries given to the Church through gifted persons. Paul, Apollos, Peter—each was different, each had his own particular gift and ministry, each was there for the common good. So it is with our pastors, teachers, administrators, counselors—each is God's gift to the Church. Rather than pit one against the other, or divide around their persons, we ought to thank God for the contribution that each makes to the Body of Christ.

Endnotes

1. I am indebted to J. Sidlow Baxter, *A New Call to Holiness* (Grand Rapids, MI: Zondervan Publishing House, 1973), 193, for this definition of the "flesh." He states that the flesh is "the animal and selfish inclination, predisposition, *propensity* within us . . . inhering in and coextensive with our moral nature."

2. I have based this exposition on Paul's use of two words here that are both rightly translated in the King James Version "carnal" (fleshly). In verse 1, he calls the Corinthians *sarkinoi*; in verse 3, he calls them *sarkikoi*. While Kittel, vol VII, p. 144, thinks the two words are used interchangeably, others like Leon Morris, p. 62, think there is a subtle difference in meaning. *Sarkinos* has no blame attaching to it due to the infancy of the believer, while *sarkikos* describes one who has been Christian for years, now knows better and is blameworthy. Richard Trench, *Synonyms of the New Testament* (Grand Rapids, MI: William B. Eerdmans Publishing Company, 1948), 272, posits much the same thought—"When Paul says of the Corinthians (3:1) that they were *sarkinoi*, he finds serious fault indeed with them; but the accusation is far

less serious than if he had written *sarkikoi* instead. He does not hereby charge them with positive active opposition to the Spirit of God . . . but only that they were intellectually as well as spiritually tarrying at the threshold of the faith. . . . He goes on indeed at verses 3 and 4 to charge them with the graver guilt of allowing the *sarx* [flesh] to work actively, as a ruling principle in them; and he consequently changes his word. They were not *sarkinoi* only, for no man and no church can long tarry at this point, but *sarkikoi* as well and, as such, full of 'envying and strife and divisions.' " This, says Barret, p. 81, is "self-centered, self-contained, self-directed."

3. See Ephesians 2:1-3, where Paul describes a believer's pre-Christian life as being one of "gratifying the cravings of our sinful nature."

4. See Romans 6:16-19 and Galatians 5:16-18 for further clarification of the concept of "yielding" to one or the other.

5. Kittel, vol. II, 5

6. Morris, 65

7. There are two Greek words for "temple," the one (*hieron*), includes all the temple precincts, and the other (*vaos*), the word used here, which denotes the sanctuary proper in which God dwells.

8. Philippians 2:9

9. 1 Corinthians 15:28

10. Colossians 3:5

11. Matthew 5: 29-30

12. Calvin, p. 137, has this wisdom concerning the inadequate pastoral work—". . . by wood, hay and stubble, is meant doctrine not answering to the foundation, such as is forged in men's brain, and is thrust in upon us as though it were the oracles of God. For God will have His Church trained up by the pure preaching of His

own word, not by the contrivances of men, of which sort also is that which has no tendency to edification, as for example curious *questions* (1 Timothy 1:4), which commonly contribute more to ostentation, or some foolish appetite, than to the salvation of men."

CHAPTER 5

Reproving a Gross Sin

1 Corinthians 4

So then, men ought to regard us as servants of Christ and as those entrusted with the secret things of God. Now it is required that those who have been given a trust must prove faithful. I care very little if I am judged by you or by any human court; indeed, I do not even judge myself. My conscience is clear, but that does not make me innocent. It is the Lord who judges me. Therefore judge nothing before the appointed time; wait till the Lord comes. He will bring to light what is hidden in darkness and will expose the motives of men's hearts. At that time each will receive his praise from God.

Now, brothers, I have applied these things to myself and Apollos for your benefit, so that you may learn from us the meaning of the saying, "Do not go beyond what is written." Then you will not take pride in one man over against another. For who makes you different from anyone else? What do you have that you did not receive? And if you did receive it, why do you boast as though you did not?

Already you have all you want! Already you have become rich! You have become kings—and that without us! How I wish that you really had become kings so that we might be kings with you! For it seems to me that God has put us apostles on display at the end of the procession, like men condemned to die in the arena. We have been made a spectacle to the whole universe, to angels as well as to men. We are fools for Christ, but you are so wise in Christ! We are weak, but you are strong! You are honored, we are dishonored! To this very hour we go hungry and thirsty, we are in rags, we are brutally treated, we are homeless. We work hard with our own hands. When we are cursed, we bless; when we are persecuted, we endure it; when we are slandered, we answer kindly. Up to this moment we have become the scum of the earth, the refuse of the world.

I am not writing this to shame you, but to warn you, as my dear children. Even though you have ten thousand guardians in Christ, you do not have many fathers, for in Christ Jesus I became your father through the gospel. Therefore I urge you to imitate me. For this reason I am sending to you Timothy, my son whom I love, who is faithful in the Lord. He will remind you of my way of life in Christ Jesus, which agrees with what I teach everywhere in every church.

Some of you have become arrogant, as if I were not coming to you. But I will come to you very soon, if the Lord is willing, and then I will find out not only how these arrogant people are talking, but what power they have. For the kingdom of God is not a matter of talk but of power. What do you prefer? Shall I come to you with a whip, or in love and with a gentle spirit?

A critical spirit is terribly destructive when it inhabits the life of a church. It finds fault with everything and everyone, from the way the choir is gowned to the content and delivery of the pastor's sermon. It makes unkind, judgmental comparisons among Christian workers, often based on traits over which the laborers have no control. It exalts itself by putting others down. It spreads dissatisfaction and murmuring among the members and can sweep through an assembly like wildfire when allowed to go uncrucified.

The root of such faultfinding is the sin which God always resists—pride. A proud man exalts himself, his opinions, his tastes, his convictions above those of others—-whom he is sure do not have his correct insights into reality. Consequently he cannot fit happily into the fellowship.

Such was the condition of the worldly-wise Corinthian church. In chapter 4 in his final censure of their fleshly divisions, Paul rebukes the proud, critical spirit that had greatly contributed to their jealous quarreling.

The Reason for the Reproof (4:1-5)

Paul had been severely and unfairly censured by some in the church of God in Corinth. If we assume that Second Corinthians is written, at least in part, to answer some of these criticisms, we may infer what sort of things were being said about him. It was said, for example, "You can't trust Paul's word. He promises one thing and does another. Why did he change his itinerary?"[1] Others said, "He came to Corinth with no letters of commendation."[2] Still others said, "He writes impressive letters, but he is anything but impressive in person, and his speaking amounts to nothing."[3] And since he made no charge for his preaching, as Greek orators did, some said he was not worth listening to,[4] while still others accused him of getting rich by dipping into the offering he was collecting for the church in Jerusalem.[5]

It is as popular today as it was in Paul's Corinth to denigrate leadership, whether it be educational, governmental or religious. A large percentage of pastors come to the end of their ministry with a low sense of self-esteem, so deeply have the cutting criticisms they endured sunk into their consciousness. Some leave the ministry to escape the stress. One pastor told me he feels his ministry is totally unappreciated. The secular community considers it to be of no real value, and some of the church elders verbally abused him. Such pastors need all the loving affirmation the church can give.

The devil sits on the shoulder of many a preacher when he is feeling low and whispers discouraging lies into his disheartened ear. Unless that preacher possesses an outlook that takes him beyond this present age, he might agree with the devil and abandon the ministry. A man of lesser caliber than Paul might have thrown in the towel in the face of such unjust attacks. Some would have said, "If this is all I get for the hard work, love and care I've invested in these people, forget it. I don't have to put up with this!"

Not Paul. His response to those who sat in judgment on him (4:1-5) was: "Apollos and I are servants of Christ and stewards of the gospel. As a steward, my first responsibility is to be a person of integrity whom the Master can trust completely to fulfill the duties entrusted to me. I have a clear conscience as far as my ministry is concerned, and therefore your unjust criticism (or for that matter any praise I might receive from men) is of no account to me. The truth is I don't even trust myself to be my own judge. I will wait until the day when Christ comes. He will judge my actions and motivations and grant me an appropriate reward."

When a minister of the Word of God has his focus on the judgment seat of Christ, where he knows he will give an account of his ministry before Him who discerns all things perfectly, he can discount the biased criticisms of others. He knows he will not be judged for his eloquence, nor his philosophical rectitude, his scholarly prowess or whether he has pleased everybody, but for his faithfulness to his calling.

John Calvin has an appropriate comment for pastors who are going through what Paul experienced:

> . . . it is the part of a good pastor to submit both his doctrine and his life for examination to the judgment of the Church, and that is the sign of a good conscience not to shun the light of careful inspection. . . . But when a faithful pastor sees that he is borne down by unreasonable and perverse affections, and that justice and truth have no place, he ought to appeal to God, and betake himself to His judgment seat, regardless of human opinion. . . .[6]

True, the pastor is not to be put on a pedestal and exalted. But it is also true that he is one of the risen Christ's gifts to the church, deserving the fervent prayers and courteous respect due to a servant of the Lord, called to feed God's flock. His sermons are for better use than "to furnish material for a little discussion and pleasant exercise of the critical faculty."[7] Today when the world is so contemptuous of the Church and so disrespectful of its pastors, it behooves congregations to take to heart Paul's word (4:5), "Therefore judge nothing before the appointed time; wait till the Lord comes."

The Nature of the Reproof (4:6-7)

One problem in the Corinthian assembly is that they were not thinking biblically. Paul has shown, by using himself and Apollos as examples, what is biblical thinking concerning the nature of ministers and ministry (3:5-9), the importance of good stewardship in fulfilling one's calling (4:1-2), the recognition that only God can properly judge a person's work (4:3-5) and the futility of man's pre-judging (4:5).

Now he urges the church to do as he and Apollos do—that is, not to go beyond the "what is written" (4:6), but to think biblically in their attitude to their teachers. When their thinking coincides with Scripture, they will find no place for being "puffed up" with pride for one minister against another.

The Christian community has no room for fleshly pride of position or person. Paul drives this home by asking three rhetorical questions. (1) "For who makes you [singular] different from [or who makes you superior to] anyone else?" The implied answer is "Certainly not God, for in His sight we are all just pardoned sinners." (2) "What do you have that you did not receive?" The implied answer is "Absolutely nothing." Whether it is eternal life, the fruit of the Spirit (Christian disposition), giftedness for particular ministry or natural talent—all we have comes from the gracious and wise provision of God. (3) "And if you did receive it, why do you boast as though you did not?" Boasting is a worldly trait that the Corinthians were manifesting, which assumes that I am what I am by my own power and wisdom. Such an attitude is out of place considering that all we are and have is a free gift from our gracious God. The prophet Jeremiah reminds us of the Word of the Lord:

> Let not the wise man boast of his wisdom or the strong man boast of his strength or the rich man boast of his riches, but let him who boasts boast about this: that he understands and knows me, that I am the LORD, who exercises kindness, justice and righteousness on earth, for in these I delight.[8]

It is important for God's people to learn to think biblically by soaking our minds in the Scriptures. Paul exhorted believers, "Let the word of Christ dwell in you richly as you teach and admonish one another with all wisdom, and as you sing psalms, hymns and spiritual songs with gratitude in your hearts to God."[9] What we sing goes deeper into our consciousness than what we speak. This attaches great importance to the contemporary custom in many churches of singing the Scriptures, thus molding our thought patterns with the Word of God.

The Sternness of the Reproof (4:8-13)

In a stinging irony, Paul illustrates through the Corinthian church some of the characteristics of the monstrous sin of spiritual pride.

1. A spiritually proud person has no sense of hunger for more of God or a deepening of the spiritual life (4:8a). He presumes that he has reached the highest echelon of godly development. But since "hunger" is a prerequisite for any deeper walk with the Lord, he will not go further in Christian experience and misses the blessing promised by Jesus to those who "hunger and thirst for righteousness."[10]

2. A spiritually proud person is not teachable (4:8b).[11] He can learn nothing from the divines of the past or from contemporary teachers, nor does he respect the faithful ministry of the pastor to whom he listens week by week. His narrow mind is closed to any interpretation of Scripture that contradicts his own.

3. A spiritually proud person is self-deceived (4:8c). He is actually far from the spiritual "kingship" he imagines himself to have gained.

4. A spiritually proud person shuns the kind of suffering for Christ that true disciples have sometimes experienced (4:9-13).

In vivid language, Paul describes the sort of existence that he and the other apostles endured, compared to the proud Corinthian church. Each day in the providence of God, their lives were in danger of death;[12] they were, in the eyes of the world, a sorry spectacle; they appeared to the worldly-wise as fools; they sensed their own great weakness; they were disgraced and discredited; they lacked food, clothing and shelter; like slaves, they were brutally handled;[13] they were treated like "the scum of the earth."[14] But they followed the example of their Lord, patiently enduring the wrongful treatment and blessing their persecutors, likely counting themselves honored to have suffered for Christ's sake.

In glaring contrast to the apostles' experience, the church in Corinth proudly clutched their dignity and sought to maintain a reputation for "wisdom" and strength, living in their own eyes as rich kings. So extreme was their spiritual pride that their values were the opposite of Paul's, so he had to give them a sharp admonition.

The Fatherliness of the Reproof (4:14-21)

As children delight in imitating their fathers, Paul calls on the Corinthians (whose spiritual father he was through the gospel) to imitate him in his self-sacrificial and humble spirit. It is so vital that they do this that he sends his faithful son in the faith, Timothy, to remind them of how he lived and that he is not requiring something of them that he does not require of all the churches.

While he was with them, Paul had evidently "kept his hand on the development of the church and, against pressure, had prevented some of its members from running wild. When his back was turned, their freedom became license; in his absence they became so used to pleasing themselves without restraint that they overlooked the possibility of his return."[15]

But Paul promises that in God's timing he will surely revisit their assembly and discover the true spiritual condition of its members. It is up to the church to decide what feature of fatherly behavior they want him to manifest. If they take his letter to heart and repent, he will express his love to them in gentleness. If they ignore his admonition, he will express his love in sternness, ready to reprimand and censure. The choice is theirs.

True love (*agape*) asks, "What is the real need of the people I love?" Love seeks, if possible, to meet that need. It gives itself up for the well-being of others. So whether a father consoles and comforts his child to take away some hurt or punishes him in order to teach obedience, the father's actions are loving, though that love is manifested in differing ways. The same is true for a pastor. I have had occasion to show love by comforting the grieving, affirming the uncertain or encouraging the downhearted. But I have also had to show a "tough" love by reproving and rebuking.

I recall sitting across my desk from a husband who kept arguing that his wife was the cause of all their marital problems. It was obvious he was more of a problem than she, but he could not or would not see it that way. Finally I gently said to him, "My friend, you are one of the most obstinate men I have ever met." He left the office immediately, angered that I should speak to him in this way. But he was in church the following Sunday, shook my hand at the door and remarked, "You are the first preacher who has ever had the courage to tell me the truth about myself!" True *agape* love must sometimes risk losing in order to win. So it was with Paul in his relationship to the Corinthians.

At this point the apostle has concluded his efforts to repair the divisions in the Corinthian church. He will turn now to other problems necessitating loving discipline.

Conclusion

What compelling truths does the Holy Spirit convey to us today? Paul reminds discouraged pastors on the brink of giving up because of unfair, unfounded criticism that it is God who judges their work, that they need take no heed to the destructive tongues of fleshly people.

To the proud and self-satisfied who, like the Corinthians, are deceived into believing they are further advanced spiritually than they really are, Paul's somewhat biting fatherly rebuke of verses 8 through 13 strikes home.

Commenting on these verses, Marcus Dods describes the condition of the Corinthian church and compels us to evaluate the extent of our yieldedness to God:

> Already the Corinthians were accepting that pernicious conception of Christianity which looks upon it as merely a new luxury, that they who are already comfortable in all outward respects may be comforted in spirit as well and purge their minds from all anxieties, questionings and strivings. They recognized how happy a thing it is to be forgiven, to be at peace with God, to have a sure hope of life everlasting. For them the battle was over, the conquest won, the throne ascended. As yet they had not caught a glimpse of what is involved in becoming holy as Christ is holy, nor had they steadily conceived in their minds the profound inward change which must pass upon them. . . . Are there none still who listen to Christianity rather as a voice soothing their fears than as a bugle summoning them to conflict. . . . Paul does not summon the whole

Church to be homeless, destitute, comfortless, outcast from all joy. . . . He means that there is not one standard of duty for him and another for us. All is wrong with us until we be made somehow to recognize, and make room in our life for the recognition, that we have no right to be lapping ourselves round with all manner of selfish aggrandizement while Paul is driven through life with scarcely one day's bread provided. . . . If we be Christ's, as Paul was, it must inevitably come to this with us: that we cordially yield to Him all we are and have. . . .[16]

The deeper Christian life calls all God's people to a life entirely surrendered to Him—a life set apart wholly for Christ's use, empowered by the indwelling Holy Spirit.

Endnotes

1. See 2 Corinthians 1:23-2:1

2. See 2 Corinthians 3:1-3

3. 2 Corinthians 10:10

4. 2 Corinthians 11:7

5. 2 Corinthians 8:20-21

6. Commentary, 152.

7. Marcus Dods, *The First Epistle to the Corinthians* (New York: Hodder and Stoughton, n.d.), 100.

8. Jeremiah 9:23-24

9. Colossians 3:16

10. Dr. A.W. Tozer in *The Pursuit of God* (Harrisburg, PA: Christian Publications, Inc., 1948), p. 15ff bemoans this inappropriate lack of spiritual hunger. I quote him at length:

   To have found God and still to pursue Him is the soul's paradox of love, scorned indeed by the too-easily satisfied religionist, but justified in happy experience by the children of the burning heart . . . .

Come near to the holy men and women of the past and you will soon feel the heat of their desire after God. They mourned for Him, they prayed and wrestled and sought for Him day and night, in season and out, and when they had found Him the finding was all the sweeter for the long seeking. . . .

How tragic that we in this dark day have had our seeking done for us by our teachers. Everything is made to center upon the initial act of "accepting" Christ (a term, incidentally, which is not found in the Bible) and we are not expected thereafter to crave any further revelation of God to our souls. We have been snared in the coils of a spurious logic which insists that if we have found Him we need no more seek Him. This is set before us as the last word in orthodoxy, and it is taken for granted that no Bible-taught Christian ever believed otherwise. Thus the whole testimony of the worshiping, seeking, singing Church on that subject is crisply set aside. The experiential heart-theology of a grand army of fragrant saints is rejected in favor of a smug interpretation of Scripture which would certainly have sounded strange to an Augustine, a Rutherford or a Brainerd.

11. I base this observation on Calvin's interpretation (p. 160) of the phrase in the NIV, "and that without us!" He interprets Paul as saying, "For Apollos and I are now esteemed nothing by you, though it is by our instrumentality that the Lord has conferred everything upon you. What inhumanity there is in resting with self-complacency in the gifts of God, while in the meantime you despise those through whose instrumentality you obtained them."

12. The phrase "on display at the end of the procession" recalls what was called by the Romans, a "Triumph." A

conquering general would lead a march home displaying the trophies of his victory. At the very end of the procession would come a group of captives who were doomed to die. See Barclay, p. 40, for a fuller description of a Roman Triumph.

13. The Greek word *kolaphidzomai* was used to describe the beating of a slave. It is used in Matthew 26:67 of the striking with their fists that Jesus received at the hands of the priests.

14. According to Kittel, vol. III, p. 430, the *perikatharmata* (NIV "scum") was a term of contempt for the unworthy and destitute; it also referred in the pagan world to what was thrown out after a human sacrifice was made as an expiatory offering. The people chosen to be sacrificed were those who could most easily be spared, the meanest and most worthless in the community (Morris, p. 82).

15. Barrett, 117.

16. *The First Epistle to the Corinthians* (New York, NY: Hodder & Stoughton, n.d.), 107f.

CHAPTER 6

Applying Church Discipline

1 Corinthians 5

It is actually reported that there is sexual immorality among you, and of a kind that does not occur even among pagans: A man has his father's wife. And you are proud! Shouldn't you rather have been filled with grief and have put out of your fellowship the man who did this? Even though I am not physically present, I am with you in spirit. And I have already passed judgment on the one who did this, just as if I were present. When you are assembled in the name of our Lord Jesus and I am with you in spirit, and the power of our Lord Jesus is present, hand this man over to Satan, so that the sinful nature may be destroyed and his spirit saved on the day of the Lord.

Your boasting is not good. Don't you know that a little yeast works through the whole batch of dough? Get rid of the old yeast that you may be a new batch without yeast— as you really are. For Christ, our Passover lamb, has been sacrificed. Therefore let us keep the Festival, not with the old yeast, the yeast of malice and wickedness, but with bread without yeast, the bread of sincerity and truth.

I have written you in my letter not to associate with sexually immoral people—not at all meaning the people of this world who are immoral, or the greedy and swindlers, or idolaters. In that case you would have to leave this

> *world. But now I am writing you that you must not associate with anyone who calls himself a brother but is sexually immoral or greedy, an idolater or a slanderer, a drunkard or a swindler. With such a man do not even eat.*
>
> *What business is it of mine to judge those outside the church? Are you not to judge those inside? God will judge those outside. "Expel the wicked man from among you."*

The ever-so-practical Apostle James tells us that "where you have envy and selfish ambition, there you find disorder and every evil practice."[1] It should not surprise us, then, that having dealt with the proud and contentious spirit prevalent in the Corinthian church, Paul now has to focus attention on specific instances of fleshly corruption and litigation countenanced within the assembly.

The Need for Discipline (5:1-2a)

We need to be clear about the situation being described here, since Paul's solution may seem drastic. This was an instance of sexual immorality exceeding even the bounds of pagan propriety. Sexual immorality pervaded Corinthian society; the heathen did not know the meaning of the word "chastity," taking their pleasure when and where they wanted it.

But even heathen Corinth had limits. Paul describes what is taking place as "a kind (of immorality) that does not occur even among pagans" (5:1).[2] This was evidently a case of incest—a professing Christian cohabiting with his stepmother. While such a thing was known in pagan society, it was generally frowned upon.

This is not a case of a man or woman caught in a reckless moment of sexual passion. Paul does not propose the excommunication of a member who has fallen momentarily into sin and is penitent. He will speak plainly in chapter 6 about fornication as a sin against the temple of the Holy Spirit, but he does not command expulsion for each instance of fornication, as sinful as that may be.

I recall a Christian teenager, a member of the church youth group, who found herself pregnant. The matter was brought before the elders, and one or two felt the instruction of First Corinthians 5 should be applied to her case. Wiser heads prevailed, and the girl, who was heartbroken and deeply repentant, was kept within the loving discipline of her church. Her experience became an occasion for wise and firm counseling of the rest of the youth group concerning the biblical teaching of abstinence and purity.

Our text, however, describes a man living willfully, brazenly, perhaps even proudly, in an incestuous relationship—a shocking breach of God's moral law.[3] The situation is compounded by the fact that the woman was likely a heathen, since no mention is made of expelling her. Thus a member of the Corinthian church was involved with a member of the kingdom of darkness, practically ensuring that the woman herself would not become a Christian.

Furthermore, the situation had become a public scandal (5:1). As long as the church refused to exercise discipline, heathen relatives of church members would have every right and opportunity to say the Christians were more immoral than the heathen. The shameful nature of the situation would thus put a blight on the name of Christ in Corinth.

Even more serious was the church's attitude toward the situation (5:2a). Once more Paul calls them "prowd."[4] Perhaps they were so proud of their assembly that they were unwilling to concede this awful blight existed. Perhaps they prided themselves on their broad-minded tolerance of the situation. Or perhaps because of their spiritual arrogance, they had no sensitivity to the manner in which such immorality reflected unfavorably upon them. Whatever the focus of their pride, it had prevented them from taking the step they should have taken.

The Character of Discipline (5:2b-8)

The situation called for drastic procedure. The health of

the church, the eternal welfare of the sinner and the reputation of the Lord Jesus were in great jeopardy.

There must come about a *change of attitude*. Instead of being proud or "puffed up," they should have manifested deep sorrow (5:2b).[5] Their change of heart would need to encompass grief for how this sin would grieve the loving heart of their Lord, concern for the ultimate state of the sinner if he did not repent and concern for the health and testimony of the church.

This change of attitude must lead them to take a *decisive course of action*. They must "put out of (their) fellowship the man who did this" (5:2b). They must "expel the wicked man from among (them)" (5:13). Excommunication was the only appropriate action in such circumstances.[6]

Excommunicating an unrepentant sinner is not greatly understood or practiced by evangelicals today. In its early form, it usually allowed the offender to join in some parts of public worship on a level with unbaptized persons, but barred him from the sacraments. Calvin, for example, would not separate the person from hearing the preaching of the Word of God in an open worship service, since this might be the avenue to repentance. In some cases, the excommunication was for a certain period of time, and until this period was up, the banned one could not enter the church. *Anathema* represented the gravest form of excommunication. Those under this ban were cast out from the shelter of the church. In the Middle Ages, this punishment would not only affect the offender's religious standing, but could upset his position in society.[7] Punishment by excommunication was done away with in the Church of England and in the Presbyterian churches of Scotland by 1700. The Roman Catholic Church still uses it.[8]

Paul gives the church explicit instructions to follow. Notice (1) the *tenor* of the action (5:2), which is as important as the action itself. The excommunication is not to be carried out with a condemning, angry or self-righteous attitude. Rather, the picture is of a grieving family burying a loved one who has died.

As stricken as the family is, it cannot allow the body to stay in the house, lest it pollute the environment. So with tears of sorrow, the sinner is to be removed from the church lest his presence corrupt the assembly.

Notice (2) the *process* of the action. First, it is an apostolic action (5:3), a procedure taken at the command and by the authority of the apostle.

Second, it is an assembly action (5:4), not the action of the elders alone, who to be sure ought to have sought to restore the brother. It is not directly the action of Paul who commands it, but rather the action of the gathered congregation.

Third, it is savingly drastic. The man is to be "hand[ed] . . . over to Satan, so that the sinful nature may be destroyed and his spirit saved on the day of the Lord" (5:5). This probably means that he is to be sent back out into Satan's world till his immorality is satiated and loses its attraction.[9]

Fourth, it is a separating action (5:9-11). Until he repents and moves out of the incestuous relationship, no fellowship will be had with this man.[10] He cannot be made to feel comfortable, nor can the church be perceived as approving his lifestyle. As the yeast, symbolizing evil, was to be removed from Israeli households for the celebration of Passover, so the sinner's corrupting influence was to be removed so that the church would not be defiled (5:6b-8).

Notice (3) the *purpose* of the action. For the sinner, the end was his ultimate eternal salvation. If he is to be saved in the Day of the Lord, he must repent. The expulsion is intended not as punishment, but to induce, if possible, repentance. This is an action that today would be called "tough love"—a love that, however painful, thinks solely of the ultimate good of the loved one. For the corporate body, the purpose was the holiness of the church; from God's perspective, the purpose was His glory.

The Shunning of Discipline (5:9-11)

Paul concludes with a general directive concerning detachment from those professed believers who are living in sin. He observes that it is impossible to disassociate from sinners outside the assembly, since the regular course of business would necessitate such association. Furthermore, God will judge them. But when it comes to sinning "brothers," he forbids even eating with them. In this, Paul reflects the teaching of our Lord, "treat him as you would a pagan or a tax collector."[11]

I have a not-too-pleasant memory of a situation in a church I pastored. A woman active in church ministry began living common-law with an unbelieving man. The elders followed the injunctions of Matthew 18 and pleaded with the young lady to remove herself from the immoral situation. When she adamantly refused to heed their loving entreaties, the congregation was informed of the situation and asked to cease fellowship with her.[12] Many did, but others described the action as "antiquated" and "unloving."

It became clear to me that "love" was misunderstood, equated with a sentimentality that did not have the young lady's ultimate good at heart. Clear, also, was the fact that unless an assembly is characterized by a deep desire to obey the Word of God, discipline is impossible to carry out. The young lady ultimately left our church for another and remained in the relationship that dishonored the name of the Lord.

The Sequel to Discipline (2 Corinthians 2:5-11)

It appears that the excommunication of the immoral man may have had a good effect. We read in Second Corinthians:

> If anyone has caused grief, he has not so much grieved me as he has grieved all of you, to some extent—not to put it too severely. The punishment inflicted on him by the majority is sufficient for him. Now instead, you ought to forgive and comfort him, so that he will not be overwhelmed by excessive sorrow. I urge you, therefore, to reaffirm your love for him. The reason I wrote you was to see if you would

stand the test and be obedient in everything. If you forgive anyone, I also forgive him. And what I have forgiven—if there was anything to forgive—I have forgiven in the sight of Christ for your sake, in order that Satan might not outwit us. For we are not unaware of his schemes.[13]

If Paul is referring to the situation in our text, it would appear that the majority of the Corinthians had obeyed his instruction and that the man was excommunicated. As a result, the Holy Spirit used the assembly's action to work godly sorrow and repentance in the man's heart, and he put away his sin. Paul is saying to the church, "There is no sin that, if confessed and forsaken, goes beyond God's willingness to forgive. If God forgives, then we must too."

Conclusion

Sadly, sexual immorality is a growing problem in local churches. The pervasive effects of the public media that glamorizes sex and the popular playboy philosophy ("If it feels good, do it") have succeeded, more than we like to admit, in dulling our sensitivity to this sin. This produces a complacency that shows itself in an unwillingness to inform on guilty parties or to take appropriate disciplinary action. We do not want to get involved, we may fear retaliation, or we may place pride of popularity above doing the will of God.

How vital that the church believe Paul's clear word concerning the immoral works of the flesh: "I warn you, as I did before, that those who live like this will not inherit the kingdom of God."[14]

And how careful we believers must be that our reputation among unbelievers does not discredit either our Lord or His Church. The world has an unjust way of lumping us all together, so that the perceived failures of one become the failures of all.

The struggle for moral purity is ongoing for not a few sincere believers. We do not overcome immoral thought patterns or habits by focusing on promises "never to do it again." Rather, the works of the flesh are put to death by a moment-by-moment yielding to the Holy Spirit who dwells within us. A consistent and persistent filling of our minds with the Word of God is necessary if we are to have pure minds in the midst of the moral pollution around us.

Endnotes

1. James 3:16
2. James Moffatt, *The First Epistle of Paul to the Corinthians* (New York, NY: Harper and Brothers Publishers, n.d.), 54-55, has this to say:

   We need not take *unknown even among pagans* too liter-ally, any more than the language of Cicero, who, in denouncing a Roman lady's passion for her son-in-law, declared that this tie was "an unbelievable crime, unheard of except for this case." . . . Greek and Ro-man history as well as romance refer to this offense against public morals. . . . Such marriages, or illicit sexual connections [sic], were not only prohibited by Roman law, however, but reprobated by public opin-ion, although, if the man was a slave, his offense would not be heinous in the eyes of pagan society.

3. Leviticus 18:7-8—"Do not dishonor your father by hav-ing sexual relations with your mother. She is your mother; do not have relations with her.

   Do not have sexual relations with your father's wife; that would dishonor your father."

4. The expression is *pephusiomenoi este*, perfect tense, signi-fying that they were in a continuing state of being "puffed up," that is proud and arrogant.

   Barrett, p. 122, observes that the Greek permits the free translation, "Are you in these circumstances puffed up?" He comments, "Paul's words do not necessarily imply that the Corinthians were puffed up simply in regard to the act of fornication, proud that it should have happened; he may refer to their general state of inflation, a bubble that this pin at least should have pricked."

5. Kittel, vol. VI, p. 42, states that *pentheo* (NIV "filled with grief ") denotes the sorrow expressed in lamentation and tears. It does not have to be open lamentation, but neither is it quiet sorrow of heart. It is passionate grief which leads to corresponding action.

6. J. Stanley Glen, p. 75, has this insightful comment concerning the expulsion of such a man as this from the assembly:

> The sharpness of Paul's demand in what is almost a crescendo of intolerance will undoubtedly shock the modern Christian unaccustomed to the thought of expelling anyone from the church. It will savor of an arbitrary spirit that is quick to discipline but slower to understand, and for this reason less acceptable to an enlightened age. From the point of view of a so-called gospel of success, the incestuous conduct of the man would probably be regarded as sickness rather than sin. . . . Rather than admit the reality of hardened characters whose perversion defies faith and whose obduracy is better known to the legal profession, the police, the social agencies, such a gospel of success prefers to minimize sin. Theoretically this gospel holds that every problem character can be saved by a thorough effort over a sufficient period of time. On this basis the incestuous man should be permitted to remain indefinitely within the church. The hope of some benefit accruing to him by his continual presence should never be lost.

7. See Elizabeth Vodola, *Excommunication in the Middle Ages* (Berkley, CA: University of California Press, 1986) for a rather thorough treatment of the subject.

8. In Roman Catholicism, excommunication means a denial
   of the sacraments. See Kenneth Hein, *Eucharist and Excommunication* (Berne, Switzerland: Herbert Lang & Co.
   Ltd., 1973) for a detailed study in early Christian doctrine and discipline.

   Marlin Jeschke, *Discipling the Brother* (Scottdale, PA:
   Herald Press, 1972) contains helpful material on the subject of excommunication.

9. Commentators differ in their understanding of what it
   means to deliver the man to Satan. Morris, p. 88, sees in it
   the possibility of some such action as is recorded in Acts
   5, the Ananias and Sapphira judgment, or in Acts 13:8-
   11, the judgment meted out to Elymas the sorcerer.
   Calvin, p. 185, sees it to simply mean excommunication—"for as Christ reigns in the Church, so Satan reigns
   out of the Church. . . . As, then, we are received into the
   communion of the Church, and remain in it on this condition, that we are under the protection and guardianship
   of Christ, I say, that he who is cast out of the Church is in
   a manner delivered over to the power of Satan, for he becomes an alien, and is cast out of Christ's Kingdom."

   Likewise there is difference of opinion as to what "the
   destruction of the flesh" means. Snyder, p. 55, I think
   says it best: "so he can learn that his self-concern will
   only lead to deeper dissatisfaction. His flesh, his living
   according to his own personal sense of fulfillment, needs
   to reach its limit. The man needs to know he cannot live
   that way. When that happens his flesh (*sarx*) will have
   been destroyed."

10. In Titus 3:10–11, Paul forbids fellowship with a divisive
    person after two warnings if he does not repent. He says,
    "After that, have nothing to do with him. You may be
    sure that such a man is warped and sinful; he is self-con-
    demned."

11. Matthew 18:15-17. The procedure described here may
    very well be the only sort of church discipline possible

these days, since the disunifed nature of local churches makes it possible for a person "excommunicated" from one fellowship to join another church which is happy to have him!

12. This form of discipline is known as "shunning," practiced in the Anabaptist tradition. It is a strong element in the Mennonite, Brethren and Amish communities that generally continue it.

13. 2 Corinthians 2:5-11

14. Galatians 5:21b

CHAPTER 7

Settling Disputes and Keeping Pure

1 Corinthians 6

If any of you has a dispute with another, dare he take it before the ungodly for judgment instead of before the saints? Do you not know that the saints will judge the world? And if you are to judge the world, are you not competent to judge trivial cases? Do you not know that we will judge angels? How much more the things of this life! Therefore, if you have disputes about such matters, appoint as judges even men of little account in the church! I say this to shame you. Is it possible that there is nobody among you wise enough to judge a dispute between believers? But instead, one brother goes to law against another—and this in front of unbelievers!

The very fact that you have lawsuits among you means you have been completely defeated already. Why not rather be wronged? Why not rather be cheated? Instead, you yourselves cheat and do wrong, and you do this to your brothers.

Do you not know that the wicked will not inherit the kingdom of God? Do not be deceived: Neither the sexually immoral nor idolaters nor adulterers nor male prostitutes nor homosexual offenders nor thieves nor the greedy nor drunkards nor slanderers nor swindlers will inherit the kingdom of God. And that is what some of you were. But you were washed, you were sanctified, you were justified in the name of the Lord Jesus Christ and by the Spirit of our God.

"Everything is permissible for me"—but not everything is beneficial. "Everything is permissible for me"—but I will not be mastered by anything. "Food for the stomach and the stomach for food"—but God will destroy them both. The body is not meant for sexual immorality, but for the Lord, and the Lord for the body. By his power God raised the Lord from the dead, and he will raise us also. Do you not know that your bodies are members of Christ himself? Shall I then take the members of Christ and unite them with a prostitute? Never! Do you not know that he who unites himself with a prostitute is one with her in body? For it is said, "The two will become one flesh." But he who unites himself with the Lord is one with him in spirit.

Flee from sexual immorality. All other sins a man commits are outside his body, but he who sins sexually sins against his own body. Do you not know that your body is a temple of the Holy Spirit, who is in you, whom you have received from God? You are not your own; you were bought at a price. Therefore honor God with your body.

North Americans live in a litigious society. Suits arise over the most trivial matters. A woman sued MacDonald's for serving her coffee too hot—and won. Several years ago, my wife slipped and fell on stairs in the public library. A woman rushed to help her and immediately remarked, "You will sue, won't you?"

The Greeks of Paul's day were notorious for their going to law. One writer describes Athenian law (Corinth would not be very different) as follows:

> If there was a dispute in Athens, the first attempt to settle it was by private arbitrator. In that event one arbitrator was chosen by each party, and a third was cho-

sen by agreement between both parties to be an impartial judge. If that failed to settle the matter, there was a court known as The Forty. The Forty referred the matter to a public arbitrator and the public arbitrators consisted of all Athenian citizens in their sixtieth year; and any man chosen as an arbitrator had to act whether he liked it or not under penalty of disfranchisement. If the matter was still not settled, it had to be referred to a jury court which consisted of two hundred and one citizens for cases involving less than about (fifty pounds) and about four hundred and one for cases involving more than that figure. There were indeed cases when juries could be as large as anything from one thousand to six thousand citizens. . . . It is plain to see that in a Greek city every man was more or less a lawyer and spent a very great part of his time either deciding or listening to law cases.[1]

It appears that some Corinthian believers had imported these litigious tendencies into the church, brother suing brother over small matters (v. 2b). Paul is distressed over this and for good reason.

Letting the Saints Judge (6:1-11)

He begins with a strong rebuke to those who would dare take their disputes before an ungodly court of law. In the first place, considering their responsibility for judging in the age to come, they could surely discover people in their own assembly capable of just judgment (6:2-4).[2]

Paul is also distressed over the reputation of Christ if believers take petty quarrels into pagan courts where the world could see how they do *not* love one another (6:6). As with the public scandal surrounding the immoral brother's behavior, the name of Christ would be defamed and the testimony of the church rendered ineffectual.

Considering the composition of a pagan court of law, how could people who had been translated out of the kingdom of darkness into the kingdom of God consider allowing their disputes to be settled by people who walked in spiritual darkness?

And how could a court composed of the sexually immoral, idolaters (who would be demonized by their worship of idols), adulterers, male prostitutes, practicing homosexuals, thieves, greedy souls, drunkards, slanderers and swindlers (6:9–10)—how could such a court be trusted to deal in a godly way with matters brought to it by those who had been delivered from those very vices (6:11a)?

After all, the Corinthian believers had been washed from their sins through faith, symbolized in the cleansing water of baptism; they had been set apart from the pagan world unto God (sanctified); they had been fully pardoned from their past sins and treated now as though they had never sinned (justified) through the the finished work of Jesus and the instrumentality of the Holy Spirit (6:11b). Reverting to pagan practices to settle disputes would be to deny who they are in Christ.

Preferring Oneself Wronged (6:7-8)

If the Corinthian believers truly loved one another, there would be no occasion for lawsuits. A loving brother would not cheat another (6:8). Even if he had been wronged, he would not retaliate by a lawsuit, but would rather allow himself to suffer wrong than be defeated in his Christian walk (6:7). It is possible to win the suit but lose spiritually.

This truth is not taken to heart by some today. One factor in the demise of a Christian college was several lawsuits initiated by certain faculty against the administration. The open conflict eroded the weakening base of support for the institution and made a scandal out of the cause of Christ. Supporters did not know whom to side with, and the wrongness of it all left many reluctant to commit their support to a bad cause (settling a series of lawsuits). The impact was destructive of the Lord's cause, of the college and of individuals.[3]

It would be best to take to heart Paul's word to the Romans, "Do not take revenge, my friends, but leave room for

God's wrath, for it is written, 'It is mine to avenge; I will re-pay,' says the Lord."[4]

Watchman Nee[5] tells of two Christian farmers whose land was irrigated by laboriously constructed waterways. One night their unbelieving neighbor redirected water from the Christians' fields into his own. The next morning the believ-ers discovered what had been done, and their first thoughts were vengeance.

But the Holy Spirit spoke to them about the words of the Lord Jesus: "I tell you, Do not resist an evil person. If some-one strikes you on the right cheek, turn to him the other also. And if someone wants to sue you and take your tunic, let him have your cloak as well. . . . Love your enemies and pray for those who persecute you, that you may be sons of your Father in heaven."[6]

Instead of taking legal action, the Christian farmers di-verted more water to their neighbor's, much to the latter's amazement. The unbeliever was so affected by the unselfish deed that he apologized and said, "If this is Christianity, I want to hear more about it."

Honoring God with One's Body (6:12-20)

Paul now comes back to the subject of sexual immorality, which he had dealt with in chapter 5. It may seem strange that the apostle should have to plead with Corinthian believ-ers to keep themselves pure. But these folk had been saved out of raw Corinthian paganism, in which intimacy with prostitutes was not considered sinful, and a collective con-science condemning this evil had not yet been established among them. Paul, inspired by the Spirit, presses them to do three things.

First, they must rethink the rationale behind the sexually permissive lifestyle of some in the church (6:12-13). This ra-tionale consists of what appear to be two popular slogans—"Everything is permissible for me," and "Food for the stomach and the stomach for food." The first embodies a misapplication of Christian liberty; the second signifies their absorption of a secular libertine philosophy that says, "We have certain appetites, and, therefore, these may be satisfied however we choose."

Paul answers their inappropriate use of these slogans by giving them other truths they would likely concede. If you say that "everything is permissible," you must agree that not everything is beneficial (6:12a). If you think immorality is permissible, have you considered that it will have consequences that are ultimately injurious? What will an immoral lifestyle do to your marriage? What will it do to your health? What will it do to your vision of God?

If you say that everything is permissible, you must know that immorality is not an expression of your Christian liberty, but a manifestation of your bondage to your fleshly appetites (6:12b). The person who thinks he must sin in order to express his emancipation needs to know he is enslaved by his so-called freedom. Christian liberty is not freedom to do what I *want*, but freedom to do what I *ought*.

If you say that life is for the fulfilment of my stomach's urges, you must remember there is more to life than that. Your life is given to you in order to cultivate the things of God. The playboy philosophy says, "Eat, drink and be merry, for tomorrow we die." That's right—tomorrow we do die, but what you do with your body has implications for the world beyond (6:13).

Second, Paul presses them to consider the implications of their impure lifestyle. Three times he asks the question, "Do you not know?" (6:15-16, 19), in order to impress upon them three momentous conclusions. First, by availing themselves of the prostitutes so numerous in Corinth, they are in reality giving to harlots that which belongs to Christ, thus degrading the Head of the Church. Unthinkable! Second, they are despising the institution of marriage by transferring to prostitutes the "one flesh" principle, which the Word of God applies solely to the marriage relationship. Third, they are desecrating the temples of the Holy Spirit (their bodies) by using them for purposes foreign to God's purposes.

Finally, Paul presses them to honor God, who purchased them at great price to be His own special people. Paul could say the same to the Corinthians as he said to believers in another city:

> I urge you, brothers, in view of God's mercy, to offer your bodies as living sacrifices, holy and pleasing to God—this is your spiritual act of worship. Do not conform any longer to the pattern of this world, but be transformed by the renewing of your mind.[7]

It is heartening to hear of hundreds of Christian youth who, despite ridicule and mockery, are honoring God by pledging themselves to remain virgins until marriage.[8] They are to be heartily commended. They can know that the living Christ will enable them to keep their vow as they daily yield to His Spirit of purity.

Conclusion

The passage encourages believers to nourish holiness. In both parts it calls upon believers to resist allowing either a litigious or a libertine spirit—both so characteristic of this world's mindset—to influence our thinking and behavior. It is not the work of the Holy Spirit to prompt a brother to defend his rights by going to court against his brother. Nor is it His work to inspire parishioners to sue their churches, a practice too common even among evangelicals. If we desire to be Christ's disciples, we must exemplify His spirit and obey His words.

The text also calls us to resist the hedonistic spirit of the age—"If it feels good, do it." Rather, our motto ought to be, "If it *is* good, do it." Scripture instructs us:

> Do not let sin reign in your mortal body so that you obey its evil desires. Do not offer the parts of your body to sin, as instruments of wickedness, but rather offer yourselves to God, as those who have been brought from death to life; and offer the parts of

your body to him as instruments of righteousness. For sin shall not be your master, because you are not under law, but under grace.[9]

We must remember that our bodies are the sacred temple of the Holy Spirit of Christ. To sin sexually is to sin against that precious temple, and against the Christ who inhabits it. Let us "put to death . . . whatever belongs to (our) earthly nature: sexual immorality, impurity, lust, evil desires and greed, which is idolatry."[10] Let us show that we are sons of God by being led by the Spirit of God.[11]

Endnotes

1. William Barclay, 49-50.
2. The NIV translation of 6:4, ". . . appoint as judges even men of little account in the church," seems to make Paul insinuate that there are some church members who are second class. Surely Paul would never say such a thing. A better translation would ask the question, "Do you appoint as judges men who have no standing in the church?"—referring to pagan judges. See Barrett, 137.
3. Firsthand account of the progressive demise of Kings College, Briarcliff Manor, NY, closed in 1994.
4. Romans 12:19
5. *Twelve Baskets Full* (Kowloon, Hong Kong: Living Spring Press, 1966), 42-44.
6. Matthew 5:38-45
7. Romans 12:1-2
8. Robert Schuller honored those of his congregation who had signed such a pledge by calling them to the front of the Crystal Cathedral during a Sunday morning service.
9. Romans 6:12-14
10. Colossians 3:5
11. Romans 8:14

CHAPTER 8

Marrying or Remaining Single

1 Corinthians 7

Now for the matters you wrote about: It is good for a man not to marry. But since there is so much immorality, each man should have his own wife, and each woman her own husband. The husband should fulfill his marital duty to his wife, and likewise the wife to her husband. The wife's body does not belong to her alone but also to her husband. In the same way, the husband's body does not belong to him alone but also to his wife. Do not deprive each other except by mutual consent and for a time, so that you may devote yourselves to prayer. Then come together again so that Satan will not tempt you because of your lack of self-control. I say this as a concession, not as a command. I wish that all men were as I am. But each man has his own gift from God; one has this gift, another has that.

Now to the unmarried and the widows I say: It is good for them to stay unmarried, as I am. But if they cannot control themselves, they should marry, for it is better to marry than to burn with passion.

To the married I give this command (not I, but the Lord): A wife must not separate from her husband. But if she does, she must remain unmarried or else be reconciled to her husband. And a husband must not divorce his wife.

To the rest I say this (I, not the Lord): If any brother has a wife who is not a believer and she is willing to live with him, he must not divorce her. And if a woman has a husband who is not a believer and he is willing to live with her, she must not divorce him. For the unbelieving husband has been sanctified through his wife, and the unbelieving wife has been sanctified through her believing husband. Otherwise your children would be unclean, but as it is, they are holy.

But if the unbeliever leaves, let him do so. A believing man or woman is not bound in such circumstances; God has called us to live in peace. How do you know, wife, whether you will save your husband? Or, how do you know, husband, whether you will save your wife?

Nevertheless, each one should retain the place in life that the Lord assigned to him and to which God has called him. This is the rule I lay down in all the churches. Was a man already circumcised when he was called? He should not become uncircumcised. Was a man uncircumcised when he was called? He should not be circumcised. Circumcision is nothing and uncircumcision is nothing. Keeping God's commands is what counts. Each one should remain in the situation which he was in when God called him. Were you a slave when you were called? Don't let it trouble you—although if you can gain your freedom, do so. For he who was a slave when he was called by the Lord is the Lord's freedman; similarly, he who was a free man when he was called is Christ's slave. You were bought at a price; do not become slaves of men. Brothers, each man, as responsible to God, should remain in the situation God called him to.

Now about virgins: I have no command from the Lord, but I give a judgment as one who by the Lord's mercy is trustworthy. Because of the present crisis, I think that it is good for you to remain as you are. Are you married? Do not seek a divorce. Are you unmarried? Do not look for a wife. But if you do marry, you have not sinned; and if a virgin marries, she has not sinned. But those who marry will face many troubles in this life, and I want to spare you this.

What I mean, brothers, is that the time is short. From now on those who have wives should live as if they had none; those who mourn, as if they did not; those who are happy, as if they were not; those who buy something, as if it were not theirs to keep; those who use the things of the world, as if not engrossed in them. For this world in its present form is passing away.

I would like you to be free from concern. An unmarried man is concerned about the Lord's affairs—how he can please the Lord. But a married man is concerned about the affairs of this world—how he can please his wife—and his interests are divided. An unmarried woman or virgin is concerned about the Lord's affairs: Her aim is to be devoted to the Lord in both body and spirit. But a married woman is concerned about the affairs of this world—how she can please her husband. I am saying this for your own good, not to restrict you, but that you may live in a right way in undivided devotion to the Lord.

If anyone thinks he is acting improperly toward the virgin he is engaged to, and if she is getting along in years and he feels he ought to marry, he should do as he wants. He is not sinning. They should get married. But the man who has settled the matter in his own mind, who is under no compulsion but has control over his own will, and who has made up his mind not to marry the virgin—this man also does the right thing. So then, he who marries the virgin does right, but he who does not marry her does even better.

A woman is bound to her husband as long as he lives. But if her husband dies, she is free to marry anyone she wishes, but he must belong to the Lord. In my judgment, she is happier if she stays as she is—and I think that I too have the Spirit of God.

As we have seen, some in the Corinthian church had harshly and unfairly criticized their founding apostle, but others were loyal to Paul and considered his apostolic convictions authoritative. These had evidently sent him a letter posing certain questions, the answers to which the members of the assembly could not agree upon. For example, they needed Paul's wisdom concerning the ethical propriety of eating meat that had been sacrificed to idols (chapter 8). They puzzled about what some considered an unbecoming breach of traditional manners (11:1-16). The way in which the Lord's Supper was being observed caused concern among them (11:17-34). And the content and style of their worship services needed addressing (12:1-14:39).

In chapter 7, Paul begins to answer their questions, the first having to do with marriage and singleness. Is it right to marry? Is it morally better to stay single? Should a Christian who is married to a pagan remain in the marriage? Is it right for a believing couple to separate? Should a single believer marry a single pagan?

The answers may seem elementary to those of us who have had conservative biblical teaching for years. But they were not obvious to the Corinthian believers, who had not had any Christian education on the matters and who had come from backgrounds with quite different attitudes toward marriage.

Today society views sexual promiscuity, marriage and divorce through less than Christian eyes, so it is fitting to remind ourselves of the enduring truths that the Holy Spirit, through Paul, sets before us in this portion of Scripture.

Fulfilling Marital Duty (7:1-9)

To begin with, this passage teaches that there is no one lifestyle (married or single) that is spiritually or morally better. Unlike some of his contemporaries, Paul does not put down marriage.[1] In his Ephesian letter, he likens marriage to the relationship between Christ and the Church and instructs husbands and wives how to relate in a Christlike manner to one another.[2]

But Paul teaches that singleness is also good (7:1). It is not abnormal or subnormal for a person to remain unmarried. In fact, there are situations in which a single life is more advantageous than married life (7:26, 38).[3] A missionary taking on a dangerous assignment might be well advised to remain single, at least until the danger is over. And the Lord of the Church has given some individuals a gift of singleness (7:7b).[4]

So in the body of Christ, it is inappropriate and unloving to make jokes about "old maids," "leftovers," "unclaimed blessings" or "men who aren't men." Such remarks come from people who may never have thought about the pain and heartbreak some singles have experienced in matters of love, or that they may even be making fun of the revealed will of God for someone.

Paul sees an advantage to marriage in a society polluted with sexual immorality (7:2). Within the marriage relationship, it is important that husband and wife give themselves fully to each other (7:3). Unlike some kinds of Puritanism, the Bible position is clear: There is absolutely nothing at all unwholesome or unclean about sexual intimacy within marriage (7:4). The "act of marriage" accomplishes not only the procreation of children, but also deepens the love of the couple for one another, provides mutual pleasure and is often a means of relieving physical tension. Only if each partner agrees should sexual intimacy be temporarily ceased for spiritual reasons (7:5). So while the apostle sees advantages in singleness, he would rather have marriage than a burning passion that may lead to immoral sexual behavior (7:9).

Remaining Permanently Together (7:10-11)

It is God's intention that a marriage should be permanent. Paul wants his readers to know that on this point the Lord Jesus Himself has spoken (7:10).[5] Here is Christ's ordered arrangement for marriage—"a wife must not separate from her husband (7:10b). . . . A husband must not divorce his wife" (7:11b). Christian couples, says Paul, must plan for permanence in their marriage. Their union is not based on mutual selfishness, but on Christ's love placed in their hearts by the Holy Spirit. They are not to be influenced by the

customs of pagan society, but by the explicit command of
the Lord, whom they desire to please.

Someone may say, "What if my spouse changes later? What
started out for 'better,' has become 'worse.' Our marriage has
turned sour. He/she's not the same person I married. We are no
longer compatible. Are we not now free to divorce and find
new compatible partners?" The answer is that the Scripture
does not say, "If you have a poor marriage you are free to divorce." Or, "Wives, stay with your husbands as long as the relationship is to your liking." Or, "Husbands, live with your
wives as long as they continue to measure up to all your expec-
tations." Nowhere are we given that license.

The Bible prefers and describes a good marriage and instructs believers how to have one. But a poor marriage is still
a marriage. And believers are called to turn a miserable relationship into a happy one through repentance, forgiveness
and reconciliation. Permanence is the goal, the ideal. So after
they have prayerfully and thoughtfully entered into marriage, believers burn all bridges, seal all exits and learn to
grow in love and understanding. They assume that all problems will be solvable when Christ is in control of the marriage.

But now, having stated the rule, Paul has something to say
about exceptional circumstances (7:11). Thank God for the
ideal rule. But He understands that this is a fallen world in
which there may have to be allowance for exceptions. There
is an ideal world but there is also a real world where the
ideal may no longer be possible. God, who loves sinners,
makes provision where the ideal does not exist.

See how Paul graciously and lovingly approaches the
problem situations. The rule is clear: "A wife must not separate from her husband." But there may be situations where
separation is unavoidable, so Paul goes on to say, "but if she
does, she must remain unmarried or else be reconciled to her
husband." Paul does not say, "If she does, she has sinned,"
or, "let her be removed from the fellowship." Separation
may be the only thing she can do.

What circumstances might necessitate separation? I hesitate to even suggest these, lest I be perceived as encouraging divorce. But it is possible to conceive of a situation in which it would be dangerous to the wife's life to remain with a violent husband. Sadly, wife beating is not totally unknown among church members. It might be conceivable that a husband, in a backslidden, rebellious condition, could become so insanely overbearing, so outrageously cruel that to live with him in peace is no longer possible. A wife might very well need to separate from a husband who lived in unrepentant and continuing immorality; or who suffered from contagious venereal disease; or was guilty of incest; or who refused to support his family; or who abandoned her. Let those who have never lived in such circumstances be slow to judge.

Sometimes, under certain circumstances, a planned "temporary separation" of the wife from her husband brings wholesome results in the husband. I once counseled a wife whose husband was unbearably cruel to leave the home and go to a shelter for battered wives. Her husband had been physically beaten as a boy and, full of rage, misdirected his anger toward his family. His wife's sudden departure so jarred him that he immediately sought help in "putting off anger" and after a period of time, was reunited with his family. The same sort of temporary separation may hasten an alcoholic spouse's "reaching bottom" and prompt him to seek help.

Separation, whether temporary or permanent, creates a potentially dangerous situation. I have seen a separated wife (it could happen to a husband) find comfort on the shoulder of a charming man who "knows exactly what she's going through." Paul allows for separation in exceptional circumstances, but not remarriage. Jesus Himself has taught us that to remarry (at least while the spouse is living) is to commit adultery.

Living with an Unbeliever (7:12-16)

Another problem circumstance in Corinth is not uncommon today. Paul describes this in verses 12-16, in which he is careful to distinguish between a direct command of the Lord and his own apostolic judgment.[6] The question is whether it is right for a Christian to cohabit with a heathen spouse. Should a Christian leave such a relationship or stay in it?

Paul's answer contains three points:

(1) There is nothing unholy or unclean about a Christian spouse cohabiting with a non-Christian (7:14). We need to understand, however, that Paul is speaking here about marriages entered into before either spouse was a Christian. The Scripture clearly forbids a believer from marrying an unbeliever.[7] But where one spouse is converted later, the believer possesses an influence for God and good over the unbeliever and their children (7:14).

(2) As long as the unbelieving spouse is willing to live with the Christian, the Christian should stay in the marriage (7:12-13). It would appear in such a case that the unbeliever feels comfortable with a Christian and may even feel the same way about Christians in general.

(3) If, on the other hand, the unbeliever in the marriage desires to leave, the believer is to "let him do so." The believer is said to be "not bound in such circumstances"[8] (7:15). Were he to insist that the unbeliever remain, it is likely that their relationship would be tempestuous. And although the Christian may wish to see the unbeliever converted, there is no guarantee that this will happen (7:16).

Starting Over Again (7:17-24)

In summary, Paul sets down this policy for believers: "Each one should remain in the situation which he was in when God called him" (7:20). He should not fret about a past that cannot be changed or be bitter about his present lot in life. If he can change it for the better—well and good, but he should regard himself as a man in Christ and be content. As far as marriage is concerned, the rule is, "Stay with God in whatever marital status you were in when God saved you. Don't you be the one to move out of the marriage."

The tremendous principle implicit in verses 17-24 is that the grace of God forever blots out the sins and failures of a believer's past; in Christ, life starts all over again. If the Church of our day is to have a ministry of grace and healing to those who, because of sin, have muddled up their lives through marital infidelity before they became believers, we must let them know that God's will always begins now. "Today is the first day of the rest of your life," says the slogan. God has "swept away your offenses like a cloud, your sins like the morning mist," says the Scripture.[9]

Weighing the Alternatives (7:25-40)

Both marriage and singleness have their peculiar advantages and dangers. For example, a single person possesses a freedom from the earthly cares that accompany marriage and children (7:28b)— a freedom that permits undivided attention to the affairs of Christ's kingdom (7:32-35).

All of us know single men and women who have perceived their singleness as God's enabling them to devote themselves to a fuller life of prayer and ministry not otherwise possible. Julie Fehr, an Alliance missionary to Gabon, was one such gifted woman. Before her death in 1994, she had been responsible for the Theological Education by Extension (TEE) program for her field and was engaged in research and writing at Wheaton on the topic of kindling and nurturing missionary movements within younger churches of the developing world. Her singleness was used by God on the mission field to teach the national believers some valuable ethical lessons and enabled her to devote undivided attention to her work. She is representative of many servants of God who are positive and joyful in their single state.

But singleness has its dangers as well, including the temptation to immorality (7:2, 9). In a city so saturated with sexual permissiveness and opportunity as Corinth, such temptation would be ever present. And Paul is teaching them and us that singleness and virginity must go together.

Refraining from sexual activity before marriage is looked upon by many today as foolish and old-fashioned, but wise and desirable grounds exist for such discipline. Here are just four good reasons:

1. Virginity affirms that God has wisely ordained that sexual intercourse should be circumscribed with family responsibility. To engage in the first without the second is to bring great psychological harm to the individual and serious consequences to society.

2. Virginity cries out that there is more to life than the satisfaction of the sexual appetite. This can well afford to wait on the intellectual, emotional and spiritual development that prepares one for all aspects of marriage, including physical intimacy.

3. Virginity precludes both pregnancy before marriage and contracting sexually transmitted diseases.

4. Virginity delights to believe that God has chosen a special person for me, and in His time He will bring us together; in that context of unconditional love and publicly proclaimed commitment, and not before, I will become "one flesh" with that special person.

Marriage too has its dangers. Family responsibilities, financial pressures, anxieties and familial frictions might stifle spiritual development (7:33–34).[10] Two extremes to be avoided are neglecting family responsibilities because of a wrongly understood emphasis on "serving God" and neglecting involvement in Christian ministry because of a disproportionate emphasis on being with the family. Both need to be wisely balanced. As God and Caesar need to be paid their due, so God and family can be proportionately honored.

Conclusion

While it is true that our text may seem somewhat unnecessary to people with 2,000 years of Christian tradition behind us, it contains some important principles that need to be underscored in today's Church. For one, the Christian "single" must be careful to let the Holy Spirit produce in him or her the godly fruit of self-control. It will be of the utmost importance to discover creative ways of sublimating sexual appetite through such means as study, strenuous physical activity or Bible meditation and to resolutely set the will to remain pure.

Second, husbands and wives must learn the true nature of the kind of love that the Scripture commands in a marriage. Romantic love is obviously a desirable element. But the kind of love that makes marriage work is *agape*—unselfishly living for the good of one's spouse. One neither "falls into" nor "out of " this kind of love. To love with *agape* love is a choice of the sanctified will made possible by the indwelling of the Spirit of God who is the Source of love.

I once heard a psychologist and marriage counselor state that "most marriages are based on mutual selfishness."[11] In other words, people get married primarily for "what *I* can get out of it. Under no circumstances must marriage be allowed to interfere with my personal goals or ambitions, because the whole purpose of marriage is to contribute to my happiness." The concept of mutual submission is foreign to selfish, fallen human nature. But partners who love one another with *agape* love will desire, as much as possible, to unselfishly meet each other's real needs.

Finally, consider Paul's words in verses 29-31. He is conscious that "The world and its desires pass away, but the man who does the will of God lives forever."[12] There is a shortness, a critical uncertainty to life that should affect all our undertakings—our marriage relationships (7:29), our social and economic life (7:30), our entire worldview (7:31). In light of Christ's coming and our appearing before Him, we should live as people who, though involved in the necessary affairs of this life, are ready to leave it all in an instant. Dr. Tozer used to say that Abraham was a wealthy man, but he possessed nothing. He who has ears to hear, let him hear.

Endnotes

1. Verse 1 is by no means a put-down of the marriage relationship.

2. Ephesians 5:21-33; see also Colossians 3:18-19

3. It is difficult to say with certainty what is "the present crisis" mentioned in verse 26. Some commentators think it is the imminent second coming of Christ; others, the persecution Christians endured for their faith; others, some unknown situation prevalent in Corinth at that time.

4. Matthew 19:11-12

5. See for example Matthew 19:1-12 for Jesus' teaching on the permanence of marriage. Paul does not often quote the words of Jesus, perhaps because he was not familiar with many of them, or more likely, he only quotes them when they disagree with the thoughts prevailing in Judaism. On divorce, the school of Hillel differed from the school of Shammai, but neither agreed with Jesus. See Barrett, 162.

6. Barrett, p. 163, makes this important observation, "Paul distinguishes sharply his own judgment from a pronouncement traceable to Jesus, but this does not mean that he regards his charge here as having no authority, or even significantly less authority than that of verse 10. Jesus, whose ministry was cast almost exclusively within Judaism . . . did not have occasion to deal with mixed marriages between the people of God and others."

7. 2 Corinthians 6:14

8. It is not altogether clear whether this expression—a believer is "not bound in this case"—does or does not permit divorce and remarriage. Interpreters are found on both sides of the issue. It is, however, likely that the unbelieving spouse having left the first marriage would remarry, and thus through adultery end the first marriage, giving the believing spouse, according to Jesus words in

Matthew 19, freedom to remarry. For further helpful thought along this line, see Dr. Martyn Lloyd-Jones, *Studies in the Sermon on the Mount, Vol. I* (Grand Rapids, MI: Williamm B. Eerdmans Publishing Company, 1964), 252-261, the chapter entitled, "Christ's Teaching on Divorce."

9. Isaiah 44:22

10. Compare our Lord's teaching in the parable of the sower and the seed in Luke 8:14, where the "seed that fell among thorns stands for those who hear, but as they go on their way they are choked by life's worries, riches and pleasures, and they do not mature."

11. Dr. Henry Brandt, in a lecture delivered in Moose Jaw Alliance Church in Saskatchewan.

12. 1 John 2:17

CHAPTER 9

Giving Up One's Rights

1 Corinthians 8

Now about food sacrificed to idols: We know that we all possess knowledge. Knowledge puffs up, but love builds up. The man who thinks he knows something does not yet know as he ought to know. But the man who loves God is known by God.

So then, about eating food sacrificed to idols: We know that an idol is nothing at all in the world and there is no God but one. For even if there are so-called gods, whether in heaven or on earth (as indeed there are many "gods" and many "lords"), yet for us there is but one God, the Father, from whom all things came and for whom we live; and there is but one Lord, Jesus Christ, through whom all things came and through whom we live.

But not everyone knows this. Some people are still so accustomed to idols that when they eat such food they think of it as having been sacrificed to an idol, and since their conscience is weak, it is defiled. But food does not bring us near to God; we are no worse if we do not eat, and no better if we do.

Be careful, however, that the exercise of your freedom does not become a stumbling block to the weak. For if anyone with a weak conscience sees you who have this knowledge eating in an idol's temple, won't he be emboldened to

> *eat what has been sacrificed to idols? So this weak brother,*
> *for whom Christ died, is destroyed by your knowledge.*
> *When you sin against your brothers in this way and*
> *wound their weak conscience, you sin against Christ.*
> *Therefore, if what I eat causes my brother to fall into sin,*
> *I will never eat meat again, so that I will not cause him*
> *to fall.*

In Western democracies, everyone including the disciple of Christ has rights under the law. We have the right to possess property; to be protected from intrusion into our homes by unwanted people; if arrested, the right to a speedy and fair trial; to travel freely within the borders of our own country; and many more rights we take for granted living in a free land, like the right to follow the dictates of our own consciences.

Scripture illustrates the existence of rights. When the Apostle Paul was beaten illegally, he insisted on exercising his rights as a Roman citizen, demanding a public apology from the Philippian magistrates.[1] Even our Lord Himself alluded to His rights under Jewish law when arrested in the Garden of Gethsemane.[2] "Human rights" are precious possessions not to be regarded frivolously but protected diligently, remembering that rights always bring responsibilities.

But on occasion Christian people are called upon for love's sake to surrender their rights, as our Lord did. Scripture tells us that although He possessed the right to uninterrupted glory with the Father, He voluntarily abdicated that prerogative in order to become a man and suffer the death of the cross.[3] This is the principle Paul sets before the Corinthian church in chapter 8—there are times when rights ought to be surrendered for the ultimate good of others.

Compelled by a Local Predicament

The Gentile believers in Corinth had been saved out of a life of idolatry, an integral part of which was the consumption of food. For example, in the worship of the goddess Demeter, food was eaten from an earthen dish called a *kernos* that had several compartments that were filled with such things as seeds and grains, or liquids like honey, milk, oil or wine. Meat such as pork and cake, which represented the fertility brought to the earth by Demeter, were also eaten.

To eat this food in the temple would be to eat food sacred to the goddess and to share in the rites of her worship. Such food could also be eaten in inexpensive dining rooms (restaurants) closely associated with the temple. Though not directly related to idol worship, the food had idolatrous connotations.[4] Some believers saw no moral danger in frequenting these eating places and took advantage of such opportunities for good food and fellowship with friends. Others, particularly Jewish Christians and Gentiles who were afraid of honoring idols or being drawn back into idolatry, could not in good conscience frequent such establishments.

Furthermore, many meals in Corinthian homes included food that had been sacrificed to idols before the meal or as one of the events of the meal. For example, whenever meals marked important social transitions such as weddings or funerals; when meals marked celebrations such as birthdays, the reunion of friends, the success of adventures or simply an elaborate meal for the pleasure of guests, sacrifice and the eating of sacrificed food were likely.[5] The best meat available in the open marketplace might well be meat offered to idols.

Corinthian believers could expect to receive many invitations to occasions where idol food would be served. These presented some believers with a moral dilemma. Should they go and eat, or refuse the invitations? Peter Gooch highlights the predicament the Christians faced:

> The social consequences of refusing to eat food offered to idols would be extreme. Events of central significance to family and friends would have to be avoided. A major means of social advancement, and

the major means of the maintenance of friendships
would at the very least be awkward and difficult for
Christians. To refuse to accept food presented at a
meal, to raise questions beforehand, and to refuse
food commonly eaten by virtually all other persons in
that society would mark Christians as odd and repugnant.[6]

The questions of rights and the surrender of rights arose
out of two differing convictions regarding the eating of
idol food. Some of the more morally sophisticated members of the assembly saw no reason for not eating the food
that had been offered in sacrifice to idols. They could eat
the food "which God created to be received with thanksgiving by those who believe and who know the truth."[7] By
eating, they could avoid the contempt, ridicule and ostra-
cism that would inevitably follow a refusal to partake. In
their view, to eat this food was a legitimate right not to be
surrendered.

Other believers were sure that eating such idol food was
morally dangerous and sinful. They could not consume such
food nor, as far as they were concerned, should any other
conscientious Christian. So to eat or not to eat was the question they put to Paul in the letter he had received from
them, which he begins to answer in 8:1.

Hindered by a Loveless Knowledge (8:1-3)

These verses reflect the tension in the church between the
"weak" members (who believed that whether a person ate or
abstained was a matter of spiritual import, and who abstained because they felt doing so commended them to God)
and the "strong" (who believed that whether a person ate or
abstained was a matter of spiritual indifference).

The latter prided themselves on their "knowledge." They
were saying in effect, "Why don't these hyper-conscientious
folk get with it? Don't they know that idols have no real existence? If they'd just give it some thought, they would have

to agree with us. We obviously have the correct theological position on the matter."

The weaker members were probably just as sure that their position was correct. For them, there was no room for compromise or broad-mindedness. Anything that savored of idolatry in the slightest degree was to be avoided at all cost.

Both sides were right and wrong at the same time. They both possessed partial truth but were holding the truth in an unloving spirit. The tendency of the strong was to look down on the weak as immature. The strong were right in what they knew, but wrong in the use of their knowledge in the fellowship of the weak.

The tendency of the weak was to judge the strong as insensitive dolts. They were right in not defiling their own consciences, but wrong in attempting to impose their conscience on the consciences of all.

In Romans 14, Paul sets forth the importance of emphasizing only the essential truths of the kingdom of God: of accepting one's brothers and not causing them to stumble and of practicing what is of faith. He also describes some Christian people who tend to hold strong convictions concerning matters about which the Scriptures make no clear pronouncements—such as certain dietary concerns, the observance of sacred days and the drinking of wine. The danger is that these sincere folk might become severely judgmental of brothers and sisters with differing convictions. He exhorts his readers to "stop passing judgment on one another"[8] while being careful that one's freedom does not cause a fellow member to fall into sin.

The key to one's understanding of these peripheral matters is the truth that "the kingdom of God is not a matter of eating and drinking, but of righteousness, peace and joy in the Holy Spirit."[9] Instead of a "know-it-all" attitude, which leads to pride (8:1) and is inadequate (8:2), the believers needed to manifest a "building-up" love, which would give evidence both of their love for God and that they were truly the Lord's people (8:3).

Many years ago on the first Sunday my wife and I were entering a new pastorate, she was dressing for church and had in mind to wear one of her sets of earrings. It occurred to her that many of the folk to whom we would minister had come from a background where wearing jewelry was frowned upon. The question before her was, "Should I exercise my right to wear jewelry (she likes pretty earrings), or should I consider the feelings of those parishioners who would be offended by the sight of anything decorating an earlobe?" She decided not to wear the jewelry.

As we were leaving the sanctuary after the service, an elderly lady with tears in her eyes approached my wife and declared, "I'm so glad that our new pastor's wife does not wear jewelry." My wife was being watched!

Prompted by a Loving Concern (8:4-13)

Paul shows both strong and weak believers how to blend knowledge with love. Those with sensitive consciences (the weak) needed to consider the facts on which the strong believers based their right to eat the idol food. What does knowledge teach us? That "an idol is nothing at all in the world and that there is no God but one" (8:4). The heathen idols are wood, stone or metal, with no reality attached to them.[10] They cannot hear, see, feel, speak, know, answer prayer or affect the outcome of things. They are only so-called gods (referred to by the heathen as "lords," 8:5), and although there are many of them, believers know there is only one living God, the God and Father of our Lord Jesus Christ. Ours is the God of Creation, for whom we live;[11] our Lord is His Son Jesus Christ, the Agent of creation and the Source of our new life (8:7).

The strong believers felt that these facts should surely settle the matter. Is not an idol a neutral, meaningless, insignificant piece of wood? If the heathen choose to offer food to this "thing," what possible significance does this have for us who know the truth? It follows that we knowledgeable people have the right to eat food that has been offered to idols, whether in a temple restaurant, in a friend's home or in our own. If the weak believers really understood, they would concede that right and not stand in judgment on us.

But this is not the end of the matter. The strong, knowledgable believers needed to learn what it meant to understand and love their weaker brethren. It could very well be, says Paul, that a person with a sensitive conscience, seeing a strong believer eating idol food, would be tempted to do the same, and thus violate his own moral principles. The danger is that this could lead to his being drawn back into pagan idolatry and leaving his Christian faith altogether.[12]

So the strong believer needs to say to himself, "Yes, I have perfect liberty to eat idol food; it is my right. But what could my exercising this right do to my Christian brother or sister? It might be the cause of their being eternally destroyed. This would be a sin against Christ Himself. I had, therefore, best surrender my rights out of love for Christ and my weak fellow believers. After all, I am perfectly free not to eat!" This was Paul's personal position in the matter, and it should have been theirs as well.

There then is the Corinthian situation that called for applying the principle of surrendered rights, a principle which, as we have seen, has modern applications as well. Marcus Dods elucidates the principle as follows:

> I, as a Christian man, and knowing that the earth and its fullness are the Lord's, may feel at perfect liberty to drink wine. Had I only myself to consider, and knowing that my temptation does not lie that way, I might use wine regularly or as often as I felt disposed to enjoy a needed stimulant. I may feel quite convinced in my own mind that morally I am not one whit the worse of [sic] doing so. But I cannot determine whether I am to indulge myself or not without considering the effect my conduct will have on others. There may be among my friends some who know that their temptation does lie in that way, and

whose conscience bids them altogether refrain. If by my example such persons are encouraged to silence the voice of their own conscience, then I incur the incalculable guilt of helping to destroy a brother for whom Christ died.[13]

Conclusion

Nothing proves a believer's genuine love for the Lord and His people more than a willingness to surrender dearly held personal prerogatives. At heart is a "death to self" that touches the core of one's being. Genuine Christian love (*agape*) is willing to surrender what is most precious to a person in order to accomplish what is best for another.

Paul sums up this way of love in the following words:

> We who are strong ought to bear with the failings of the weak and not to please ourselves. Each of us should please his neighbor for his good, to build him up. For even Christ did not please himself. . . .[14]

This points us again to our Lord and Savior, whose loving behavior the Holy Spirit enables us to manifest in all our human relationships. "This," says the Apostle John, "is how we know what love is: Jesus Christ laid down his life for us. And we ought to lay down our lives for our brothers."[15]

Endnotes

1. Acts 16:37f
2. Matthew 26:55
3. Philippians 2:5-11 instructs Christians to emulate this self-sacrificial mind of Christ.
4. Peter D. Gooch, *Dangerous Food* (Waterloo, IL: Wilfred Laurier University Press, 1993), 13.
5. Ibid., 37.
6. Ibid., 46.

7. 1 Timothy 4:3

8. Romans 14:13

9. Romans 14:17

10. Paul will later remind the Corinthians (10:20) that there are demonic beings behind the idols, and that this fact should influence their attitudes toward idolatry. But that is not the point here.

11. Literally "we unto Him." The preposition translated "unto," *eis*, indicates the set of one's life. "The Christian lives for God. He lives only to do Him service." Morris, 126.

12. The question might be asked, "What should a 'strong' believer do, if he knows his behavior will not really cause a 'weak' brother or sister to apostatize from the faith, but might only offend his sense of propriety, and bring a rift in their fellowship?" In such a case, the strong believer will need to consider carefully what love would do. It is likely that he will not want to bring the slightest offense to his fellow Christian.

13. p. 187.

14. Romans 15:1-3

15. 1 John 3:16

CHAPTER 10

Modeling Christian Service

1 Corinthians 9:1-23

Am I not free? Am I not an apostle? Have I not seen Jesus our Lord? Are you not the result of my work in the Lord? Even though I may not be an apostle to others, surely I am to you! For you are the seal of my apostleship in the Lord.

This is my defense to those who sit in judgment on me. Don't we have the right to food and drink? Don't we have the right to take a believing wife along with us, as do the other apostles and the Lord's brothers and Cephas? Or is it only I and Barnabas who must work for a living?

Who serves as a soldier at his own expense? Who plants a vineyard and does not eat of its grapes? Who tends a flock and does not drink of the milk? Do I say this merely from a human point of view? Doesn't the Law say the same thing? For it is written in the Law of Moses: "Do not muzzle an ox while it is treading out the grain." Is it about oxen that God is concerned? Surely he says this for us, doesn't he? Yes, this was written for us, because when the plowman plows and the thresher threshes, they ought to do so in the hope of sharing in the harvest. If we have sown spiritual seed among you, is it too much if we reap a material harvest from you? If others have this right of support from you, shouldn't we have it all the more?

But we did not use this right. On the contrary, we put up with anything rather than hinder the gospel of Christ. Don't you know that those who work in the temple get their food from the temple, and those who serve at the altar share in what is offered on the altar? In the same way, the Lord has commanded that those who preach the gospel should receive their living from the gospel.

But I have not used any of these rights. And I am not writing this in the hope that you will do such things for me. I would rather die than have anyone deprive me of this boast. Yet when I preach the gospel, I cannot boast, for I am compelled to preach. Woe to me if I do not preach the gospel! If I preach voluntarily, I have a reward; if not voluntarily, I am simply discharging the trust committed to me. What then is my reward? Just this: that in preaching the gospel I may offer it free of charge, and so not make use of my rights in preaching it.

Though I am free and belong to no man, I make myself a slave to everyone, to win as many as possible. To the Jews I became like a Jew, to win the Jews. To those under the law I became like one under the law (though I myself am not under the law), so as to win those under the law. To those not having the law I became like one not having the law (though I am not free from God's law but am under Christ's law), so as to win those not having the law. To the weak I became weak, to win the weak. I have become all things to all men so that by all possible means I might save some. I do all this for the sake of the gospel, that I may share in its blessings.

Speaking of "rights," the other day I pulled my rather dog-eared certificate of ordination out and read it again as a matter of interest. It certified that I,

after due examination as to (my) conversion, call to preach, and doctrinal views . . . was set apart with prayer and the laying on of hands to the work of the

Gospel ministry, preaching the Word, administering the ordinances, and performing all the duties and enjoying all the privileges to which a Minister of the Gospel is called and entitled.

That last phrase struck me—"enjoying all the privileges" to which I was now entitled. I had to think for a moment about what those privileges were. There was, of course, the privilege of preaching the gospel. And the right to financial support, although over the years some parishioners had wondered about that. There was the right to be respected as a minister in my denomination. I had the privilege of using a large university library. I was glad for that.

When I first started out, my clergy status granted me a ten percent discount at the local men's clothing store. That no longer pertains, since the stores think we preachers can now afford full price. There were invitations to meals and gifts of produce, meat and eggs and a few other perks. There were indeed some privileges associated with my pastoral position. But not as many as my ordination certificate seemed to imply. They were far outweighed by the responsibilities. I discovered before many years had gone by that if I were to continue in the work of the gospel ministry, I would have to die to almost all of those privileges.

A Devoted Servant (9:1-18)

Paul had his rights and privileges too. But in exhorting the "strong" Corinthian believers to set aside their personal rights in the matter of eating idol food, he wanted them to know that he was not laying upon them a principle that he ignored in his own life and ministry. In our text, he demonstrates and defends his rights and privileges as an apostle, but declares that he has relinquished them for the gospel's sake.

He begins by setting forth his right to financial support. Evidently people in the church at Corinth were accusing the apostle of being in the ministry of the gospel just for the money. It is important that, out of love for the church, he defend against this unjustifiable criticism. They need to face up to their wrong, hyper-critical spirit and their thoughtless neglect of Paul.

The first point in the defense of this right is to remind the Corinthians that he is, in fact, a free, bona fide apostle. Like the other apostles he too had seen the Lord Jesus (9:1a). He is saying, in effect, "The risen Lord Jesus called me away from my previous life into full-time preaching of the gospel. I didn't go into it for the money, the prestige or the power. My life was suddenly interrupted one day at high noon by the glorified Christ, who called me to be an apostle. What else could I do? Furthermore, the result of my ministry has demonstrated the legitimacy of my calling. There is a church of Jesus Christ in the city of Corinth" (9:1b). Paul was sure of his vocation. He had a right, therefore, to expect financial support both for himself and a wife from the churches he had founded (9:4-6).

The second element of his defense are three down-to-earth analogies (9:7). Whether it's soldiering, seeding or shepherding, everyone who works expects to profit from his or her labor. Does anyone complain that soldiers don't have to pay for their own tickets to the war zone? Would the Defense Department say to those in uniform, "We're going overseas to battle; the airline ticket costs $800. We'll be deducting that from your next paycheck. And you'll have to pay for your own guns and training"? Of course not.

And if we were to ask a cattle farmer why he was in that business, we wouldn't expect him to reply, "Oh, just for the pleasure of it." Likewise Paul is saying, "I have a right on the grounds of common sense to make a living from my work."

But more than that, Scripture proves Paul's right to financial support. When the Law commands, "Do not muzzle an ox while it is treading out the grain,"[1] it not only applies to cattle, but to those who are in "full-time service" for the Lord (9:8-12).[2] Furthermore, the Law required that priests in the temple were to be supported by the gifts and sacrifices brought to temple (9:13). And the Lord Jesus commanded that gospel preachers be supported by their converts (9:14).[3] So to those who would deny him financial support for his work, Paul's answer is simply that on secular and biblical grounds he has every right to expect generous remuneration for his gospel ministry.

The evangelist Charles Finney makes the point that the blessing of God upon any church is vitally connected to their paying their pastor adequately.[4] He contends that a pastor should have no financial worries whatever. It has been said that a person's salary is in proportion to the value that society places upon him or her. This would explain, for example, the multi-million dollar contracts that sports heroes negotiate or the huge cost of retaining some lawyers. What value does an assembly of believers place upon their pastor and his ministry among them if he is grossly underpaid but they can pay him more? Surely Paul would have been in agreement with Finney.

Not only does Paul have a right to financial support, but he claims a right to be "free and belong to no man" (9:19). He could be referring to his status of a free man as a Roman citizen[5] or to his having been made free as a Christian.[6] To "belong to no man," however, would imply that his actions were never psychologically necessitated reactions to the demands of other people. Whatever his ministry to others, it was always dependent upon his own Spirit-guided, thoughtful, personal and free choice.[7]

Having laid claim to his rights, Paul proceeds to describe the surrender of those rights. As far as his ministry in Corinth was concerned, he had refused to accept financial support from the church (9:12b). Nor was it his intention by writing to subtly manipulate the Corinthians into paying him in the future (9:15). In view of the critical attitude of the church toward him, he chose for love's sake to give them no grounds for accusing him of being in the ministry for the money. God had called him to apostleship, and he gloried in being able to offer the gospel free of charge (9:18). If demanding his right to support would stand in the way of their responding to the gospel, then he would refuse their support.

A Deliberate Slave (9:19-23)

Not only had Paul chosen to surrender his right to financial support, but he had also chosen to abdicate his right to be free from slavery to people (9:19). Notice the paradox here. "I am free and belong to no man"; yet, "I make myself a slave to everyone." He is free not to be free. This bondage to everyone that he has chosen is not a crippling, stifling, enchainment to people's opinions or demands, nor is it a fear of what people will think. Paul is his own free man in Christ. He takes no salary, so he is under obligation to no one. He doesn't have to weigh his sermons to see if they will please the people who pay him. He has nothing to prove. He doesn't have to be successful in the eyes of men, has no image to maintain and no need to be forever explaining himself. He has no need to be anything other than what he really is. What glorious liberty! What profound integrity!

Notice the pattern of his deliberate slavery. "I have become all things to all men" (9:22). What does Paul mean by that? Is he a hypocrite—"when in Rome do as Romans do"? Paul would never allow himself that evil. Does he mean that he compromises his conscience or his standards, like a person saying, "The best way to win an alcoholic is to drink with him; or the best way to win a thief is to steal with him"? Obviously not. Paul explains and illustrates what he means in four declarations:

First, "To the Jews I became like a Jew" (9:20a). We see him doing this when he had the young man Timothy circumcised "because of the Jews who lived in that area, for they all knew that his father was a Greek."[8]

Second, "To those under the law I became like one under the law (though I myself am not under the law)" (9:20b). We see him, for example, following the suggestion of the Jerusalem elders to join four other men in a purification rite, and then, along with them, to go into the temple "to give notice of the date when the days of purification would end and the offering would be made for each of them."[9]

Third, "To those not having the law I became like one not having the law (though I am not free from God's law but am under Christ's law)" (9:21). In his relationships with heathen, he plays down all the traditions of Judaism, refusing to make issues out of points in the Mosaic law. When, for example, he preaches the gospel to the Athenian leadership in a meeting of the Areopagus, he catches their attention by referring to their "objects of worship," particularly, their altar inscribed "to an unknown god." With this as a springboard, he quotes their own poets and proceeds to proclaim the Man whom God raised from the dead.[10]

And fourth, "To the weak I became weak, to win the weak" (9:22a). His refusal to eat meat offered to idols for the sake of "weak" brothers illustrates his becoming weak for their sake.[11]

In other words, Paul seeks to get alongside anyone and everyone. The purpose of his deliberate slavery is "to win as many as possible" (9:19b); "to win those under the law" (9:20); "to win the weak" (9:22a); "so that by all possible means I might save some" (9:22). And "I do all this for the sake of the gospel, that I may share in its blessings" (9:23). In other words, Paul's goal given him by Christ is to bring people to Christ, and his "slavery" to men relates directly to his God-given goal. He brings his life under subjection to accomplishing that goal.

Paul is saying to the Corinthians, "I'll do whatever I can without compromise or disobedience to Christ in order to gain a hearing for the gospel. I'll go anywhere, accommodate myself to any situation, listen to any man to understand his point of view, get interested in his interests, make cultural adjustments—anything, if it will enhance the possibility of winning him to Christ. If he rejects the gospel, then at least I can be sure that it is the gospel that offends him and not my unwillingness to be his friend."

William Barclay describes this method of ministry as "being able to get alongside anyone." Quoting the lawyer Boswell, he calls it "the art of accommodating oneself to others." He attributes this art to Dr. Samuel Johnson (1709-1784) in these words:

> . . . not only was he a great talker, but he was also a great listener with a supreme ability to get alongside any man. A friend said of him that he had the art of "leading people to talk on their favorite subjects, and on what they knew best." Once a country clergyman complained to Mrs. Thrale's mother of the dullness of his people. "They talk of runts (young cows)," he said bitterly. "Sir," said the old lady, "Mr. Johnson would have learned to talk of runts." . . . He was a man who would have enjoyed discussing the manufacture of spectacles with a spectacle-maker, law with a lawyer, pigs with a pig-breeder, diseases with a doctor, or ships with a ship-builder.[12]

Paul practiced this art well for the sake of the gospel.

Conclusion

Although it calls us to lay down our rights for the sake of the gospel, this passage makes a powerful case for the proper financial support of those who minister the gospel. This is hard work! I have heard it said that to preach a half-hour sermon takes as much energy as a hard day's manual labor. If the work is to be done adequately, a pastor must spend much time in prayer and the study of Scripture. And there is the care of the flock, to say nothing of the fact that he is on call day or night. He has no time for another job to earn a living. A faithful congregation will see to it that he has no financial needs that give him cause for anxiety.

The other side of the coin, however, is that a faithful pastor will not do his work just for the money. The Apostle Peter exhorts pastors "not (to be) greedy for money, but eager to serve."[13] It is not likely that a Spirit-controlled servant of the Lord will be a "clock watcher," rigorously holding to a forty-hour week!

Our text also sets forth the principle of "friendship evangelism." In his humorous, but penetrating allegory, *The Gospel Blimp*, Joseph Bayly shows how much better it is to evangelize by getting socially close to one's unconverted neighbor than to engage in a sort of evangelism program that does not involve getting alongside people.[14] Dropping "gospel bombs" from a "gospel blimp" is an apt metaphor for this kind of impersonal effort. Believers who desire to be effective witnesses to Christ in our day may need to surrender their right to a self-centered independent lifestyle in order to get alongside those they would win.

Endnotes

1. Deuteronomy 25:4

2. He makes the same point in First Timothy 5:17-18, quoting the same passages from Deuteronomy and Luke.

3. See Matthew 10:10; Luke 10:7

4. *Lectures on Revivals of Religion* (Old Tappan, NJ: Fleming H. Revell Company, n.d.), 262-263.

5. Morris, 138.

6. Barrett, 210.

7. In this respect he emulated his Lord, whose own ministry was always based on Spirit-guided choices, rather than reactions to what others thought He should be doing. A good example of this is His non-response to Mary and Martha's message, "Lord, the one you love is sick" (John 11:3). Upon hearing this, "he stayed where he was two more days" (11:6). His method of ministry to the family was based not on what he knew they would expect, but upon what he knew would best glorify God.

8. Acts 16:3

9. Acts 21:23f

10. Acts 17
11. See again 1 Corinthians 8; Romans 14
12. p. 83-84.
13. 1 Peter 5:2
14. Published by Chariot Family, 1983.

CHAPTER 11

Pursuing Discipline and Carefulness

1 Corinthians 9:24-10:13

Do you not know that in a race all the runners run, but only one gets the prize? Run in such a way as to get the prize. Everyone who competes in the games goes into strict training. They do it to get a crown that will not last; but we do it to get a crown that will last forever. Therefore I do not run like a man running aimlessly; I do not fight like a man beating the air. No, I beat my body and make it my slave so that after I have preached to others, I myself will not be disqualified for the prize.

For I do not want you to be ignorant of the fact, brothers, that our forefathers were all under the cloud and that they all passed through the sea. They were all baptized into Moses in the cloud and in the sea. They all ate the same spiritual food and drank the same spiritual drink; for they drank from the spiritual rock that accompanied them, and that rock was Christ. Nevertheless, God was not pleased with most of them; their bodies were scattered over the desert.

Now these things occurred as examples to keep us from setting our hearts on evil things as they did. Do not be idolaters, as some of them were; as it is written: "The people sat down to eat and drink and got up to indulge in pagan revelry." We should not commit sexual immorality, as some of them did—and in one day twenty-three thousand of them died. We should not test the Lord as some of them did—and were killed by snakes. And do not grumble, as some of them did—and were killed by the destroying angel.

These things happened to them as examples and were written down as warnings for us, on whom the fulfillment of the ages has come. So, if you think you are standing firm, be careful that you don't fall! No temptation has seized you except what is common to man. And God is faithful; he will not let you be tempted beyond what you can bear. But when you are tempted, he will also provide a way out so that you can stand up under it.

The spiritual "father" of the Corinthian church has been answering their questions about eating food that had been sacrificed to idols. He has shown the "weaker" members on what grounds the "stronger" members feel free to partake of this perilous food and the "stronger" how love for the "weaker" would mean voluntarily sacrificing their right to eat.

Throughout his argument and especially in the light of what follows in chapter 10, one cannot help but notice the concern Paul has for the spiritual welfare of the "knowledgeable" strong members.

While he seems to support their reasoned argument in defense of the right to eat food offered to idols (8:4-6), he is concerned that the strong Corinthians grasp the truth that even they, with all their knowledge, are susceptible to being drawn back into their pagan past. Do they really understand the nature and power of idolatry? Do they understand the necessity for watchful perseverance in their Christian walk? This concern pervades the passage before us.

If Paul were alive today, he would surely be concerned about the glib "easy-believism" characteristic of much of the evangelical world. For too many, the essence of Christian faith is a one-time intellectual agreement (mistakenly called "faith") with two or three gospel verses of Scripture, followed by a coached prayer that assures the "eternal security" of the "believer." Evangelistic techniques often replace the more thorough work of the Holy Spirit in awakening, convicting and converting sinners. Nor is thought given to following after the "holiness without which no man shall see the Lord."[1]

Paul's Demanding Discipline (9:24-27)

We have seen how Paul's ministry included relinquishing certain apostolic rights. Combined with that was a meticulous self-disciplined watchfulness, which he wanted all the Corinthian believers, strong and weak, to duplicate.

He sees his self-denial as analogous to a Greek athlete's preparation for the Isthmian Games,[2] in which the one great objective of the runner or boxer was to gain the prize—a perishable pine wreath—and the honor that went with winning. For this earthly honor, he would undergo ten months of agonizingly strict training because he knew that starting the race would not necessarily mean winning.

So it is in the Christian life. Entrance into the Way does not guarantee perseverance. Paul wants us to know that winning the crown of glory necessitates a spiritually rigorous "enslavement of the body" (9:27a), akin to (as Jesus put it) "cutting off " the offending hand and "gouging out" the offending eye.[3] Paul puts it elsewhere as not letting sin "reign in your mortal body so that you obey its desires."[4]

He describes this rigorous living of the Christian life in four expressions (9:26-27):

1. Not "running aimlessly"[5] with no fixed goal. Paul knew he had not completed his course and in his Philippian letter declares: "But one thing I do: Forgetting what is behind and straining toward what is ahead, I press on toward the goal to win the prize for which God has called me heavenward in Christ Jesus."[6]

2. ". . . not fight[ing][7] like a man beating the air"[8]. . . "dealing ill-directed and ineffectual blows."[9]

3. ". . . beat[ing] [his] body . . ."[10] Paul deals ruthlessly with
   the flesh, remembering that "the [flesh] desires what is
   contrary to the Spirit, and the Spirit what is contrary to
   the [flesh]. They are in conflict with each other. . . ."[11]

4. Making his body his slave.[12] Paul uses these last two
   terms "to express the fact that his *soma* [body], with all
   that belongs to physical life, is fully and emphatically
   subordinate to his office and has a right to existence only
   in so far as it at least does not hamper him in the dis-
   charge of this office."[13]

Paul's great concern is that, having been the messenger of
the gospel to others, he would be "disqualified for the prize"
(9:27b).[14] This does not mean that he was worrying from
one day to the next lest he fall away from the faith and be
lost. He knew the One in whom he believed and was confi-
dent of Christ's keeping power. But neither did Paul believe
that one should "go on sinning so that grace may increase."[15]
He would not presume on the grace of God. He recognized
that believers are called to holiness (Christlikeness), and he
understood the desire after holiness to be a necessary mark
of the believer. This truth needs to be steadfastly proclaimed
in our churches today.

Israel's Defiant Carelessness (10:1-10)

Having set forth the indispensable importance of being
well-disciplined in his own Christian walk, Paul warns the
Corinthians not to take their ultimate salvation for granted.
He uses the sad history of the Old Covenant nation of Israel
to teach New Covenant believers what can happen when
people do not guard themselves from the temptations linked
to idolatry (10:11).

The "knowledgable" Corinthians were not taking idolatry
seriously enough because they apparently believed that participation in the Christian sacraments—baptism and the
Lord's Supper—secured them from any spiritual harm. In
this respect they were much like present-day folk who rest

in the impression that the rite of baptism or a ritualistic partaking of the eucharist secures ultimate salvation without the kind of vital faith that continually appropriates the meaning of the symbols.

Paul then informs his readers of Israel's privileges. Ancient Israel, having been "saved" out of Egypt, had also been given sacraments which were tokens of God's grace to them. They, like the Corinthians, had been baptized (10:2)[16] and had been partakers of sacramental food and drink (10:3-4a).[17] Christ had been the Rock that followed them, the Source of all the blessings the Israelites received as they journeyed.

Nevertheless (and here is the reality the Corinthians needed to take to heart), notwithstanding their sacramental advantages, most of the Israelites fell into sin and perished in the wilderness as a result of God's sentence against rebels (10:5). They were not permitted to enter Canaan, the Land of Promise.[18]

And what caused them to perish? Paul describes Israel's Perversions—five tragic failures out of their history that the Corinthians were in danger of repeating. First, they "[set their] hearts on evil things" (10:6). The allusion is to Israel's craving Egyptian food and complaining about God's simple but adequate provision of manna. God gave them the meat they lusted for, but in eating it they suffered a fatal plague that provided a name for the place where it happened—"Graves of Craving."[19]

Second, Israel reverted to idolatry (10:7). God had summoned Moses to Mt. Sinai to receive the Ten Commandments. When he failed to return, the golden calf was fashioned and an idolatrous festival ensued, resulting in God's severe judgment.[20] Paul fears that the "strong" Corinthians may be headed in the same dangerous direction.

Third, Israel was guilty of the sin of sexual immorality (10:8). The ancient record describes how the sins of idolatry and fornication are closely connected:

> While Israel was staying in Shittim, the men began
> to indulge in sexual immorality with Moabite

women, who invited them to the sacrifices to their
gods. The people ate and bowed down before these
gods. So Israel joined in worshiping the Baal of Peor.
And the LORD's anger burned against them.[21]

A fashionable cult in Corinth was the worship of Aphrodite, whose priestesses were sacred prostitutes. Going into
an idol temple might inflame sexual passion and result in immorality—the sin for which Corinth was renowned. Paul's
warning is, therefore, appropriate: Steer clear of every
source of temptation to sexual immorality.

Fourth, Israel "test[ed] the Lord" (10:9). The record tells us
that "the people grew impatient on the way; they spoke against
God and against Moses, and said, 'Why have you brought us
up out of Egypt to die in the desert? There is no bread! There
is no water! And we detest this miserable food!' "[22]

Instead of trusting in God's loving providence, they became unbelievers, doubting His purposes, plans and abili-
ties. Again they brought upon themselves God's judgment,
this time in His sending venomous snakes among them. Paul
warns the Corinthians not to test God by seeing how far
they could go in the direction of idolatry.

The last of Israel's perversions to which Paul alludes is
their grumbling (10:10a). When the twelve spies returned
from exploring Canaan, they reported "the land we explored
devours those living in it. All the people we saw there are of
great size. . . . We seemed like grasshoppers in our eyes, and
we looked the same to them."[23] The record states,

> That night all the people of the community raised
> their voices and wept aloud. All the Israelites grum-
> bled against Moses and Aaron, and the whole assem-
> bly said to them, "If only we had died in Egypt! Or
> in this desert! Why is the LORD bringing us to this
> land only to let us fall by the sword." . . . And they
> said to each other, "We should choose a leader and go
> back to Egypt."[24]

When Korah, Dathan and Abiram were judged for their opposition to Moses' leadership, we are told that "[t]he next day the whole Israelite community grumbled against Moses and Aaron."[25] Grumbling against God and His servants is a serious evil in God's eyes, bringing upon the grumblers severe judgment that Paul describes as being "killed by the destroying angel" (10:10b). Grumbling against Moses was grumbling against God, and by the same token, grumbling against Paul is grumbling against God.

Believer's Deliberate Carefulness (10:11-13)

Finally Paul advances the moral of the stories. "So, if you think you are standing firm, be careful that you don't fall!" (10:12). The overconfident "strong," "knowledgeable" Corinthians were in peril of perdition. They must learn from the example of the forefathers if they are to avoid their fathers' fate. The temptations they faced were not unique to them (10:13a). If they would but take the way out that God provided instead of looking for a way to get as close to idolatrous influences as they could, they would discover that the temptations were not beyond their ability to withstand (10:13b).

Conclusion

This passage contains vivid and commanding stories. Taken from the history of Israel, they are powerful warnings to the Corinthians and clearly serve as cautions to us who, like them, are living at the the culmination of all past ages (10:11). How dangerous, for example, for believers to become so self-assured in their faith that they lose their first love for God. They can begin to resent what they feel are "restrictions" God has placed upon their lifestyles. They become envious of the "freedom" and pleasures of the world and crave their former lifestyle, forgetting that it was an "Egyptian" bondage.

Having lost their first love, it becomes easy to allow the gods of materialism and pleasure to become the idols that backsliders worship. Idolatry makes way for sensuality; sensuality leads to unbelief. I recall some years ago having coffee with a former fellow student from Bible college, who calmly told me that he no longer believed there was a God. His loss of faith did not happen suddenly. He had allowed an immoral and sensuous mind to spoil his marriage. At the time of our conversation, he was living with another woman.

As is so often the case, "sensuality is the parent of unbelief, both because it produces a consciousness of guilt and because it blunts the spiritual discernment."[26] The mind discovers a way of dispensing with the existence of the One whose moral code it wishes to disobey. My friend had started out well but had not resisted temptation when it had made its first pleasurable approach. Let us be warned!

Endnotes

1. Hebrews 12:14. John MacArthur echoes the same concern in *The Gospel According to Jesus* (Grand Rapids, MI: Zondervan Publishing House, 1988), 182. He asks, "How does this [Jesus' teaching in Luke 13, concerning striving to enter in by the narrow gate] fit the modern notion that salvation is easy? What does it do to the popular teaching that becoming a Christian is only a matter of believing some facts, signing on a dotted line, walking an aisle, raising a hand or praying the right prayer? Could it be that many of our 'converts' are on the wrong road because they took the easy way through the wrong gate?"

2. Second only to the Olympic Games, the Isthmian Games were held every three years in Corinth.

3. Matthew 5:29-30

4. Romans 6:12

5. The word is *adelos*—"not aimlessly."

6. Philippians 3:13-14

7. The word is *pukteuo*, "to fight with the fists," "box."

8. To "beat the air," (*aera deron*) is used of unskillful boxers who miss their mark.

9. Barrett, 217.

10. *Upopiadzo* means literally "to strike under the eye, give a black eye." Symbolically it has the thought of treating roughly.

11. Galatians 5:17

12. *Doulagogeo* means "to lead into slavery," "to cause to live the life of a slave."

13. Kittel, vol. II, 280.

14. Interpreters are not at all in agreement as to the meaning of this phrase, which is the NIV translation of the word *adokimos*. For example, Leon Morris, p. 140, is quite sure that "Paul's fear was not that he might lose his salvation, but that he might lose his crown through failing to satisfy his Lord" (cf. iii:15). On the other hand, C.K. Barrett, p. 218, thinks that Paul "clearly envisages the possibility that, notwithstanding his work as a preacher, he may himself fall from grace and be rejected. . . . His conversion, his baptism, his call to apostleship, his service in the Gospel, do not guarantee his eternal salvation." Again, James Moffat, *The First Epistle of Paul to the Corinthians* (New York, NY: Harper and Brothers Publishers, n.d.), 127, defines *adokimos* as meaning "the opposite of securing one's share in the final salvation." One of the fairest and most thorough treatments of the meaning of *adokimos* is given by I. Howard Marshall, *Kept by the Power of God* (Minneapolis, MN: Bethany Fellowship, Inc., 1969), 120. He favors the idea that Paul is concerned about the loss of his salvation, but he fairly presents arguments against this position. We will never solve the problem to everyone's satisfaction. But whatever Paul meant, being "disqualified for the prize" is something to be strenuously avoided!

15. Romans 6:1ff

16. Barrett, p. 221, observes that there is some evidence that Jews regarded the passage through the Red Sea as a kind of baptism, (analogous to proselyte baptism). Morris, p. 114, states, "The experience of being guided by the cloud, and of passing through the Red Sea (Exodus 14) had the effect of uniting the people to Moses in such a way that they are said to have been *baptized unto Moses* (the Greek seems to imply a willingness to get themselves baptized in this way)." He goes on to observe that just as baptism has the effect of bringing a person under the leadership of Christ, so participation in the great events of the Exodus brought the Israelites under the leadership of Moses.

17. Key to understanding the meaning of these verses is what Paul meant in this context by the word, "spiritual" (*pneumatikos*). Edwards, p. 245, points out the two possibilities, namely, the food and drink was of supernatural origin; or the food and drink had allegorical and even sacramental significance. Morris, p. 141, thinks that the designation "spiritual" was Paul's way of noting the heavenly origin of the food. Barrett, p. 222, on the other hand thinks that by "spiritual," Paul may mean that the food and drink had a further significance in addition to their material function as food and drink for the body, or that they were symbolical, or typical of the Christian sacrament. He notes that *pneumatikos* denotes some thing or person that is the bearer or agent of the Holy Spirit (9:11; 12:1; 14:1; 15:44, 46). So, "the food and drink actually conveyed spiritual (as well as material) sustenance to the Israelites, and at the same time were used by the Spirit as visible prophecies of what was still to be established."

Dods, p. 232, is certain that "spiritual" means "sacramental," i.e., the literal food and drink continually spoke to Israel of God's nearness, and reminded them that they were His people. The manna and the water were sacraments, means of grace, given to quicken faith in God, continuous signs and seals of God's favor. Edwards, p. 245, tells us that "the Mosaic dispensation had real sacraments, and not mere types of sacraments."

18. See Numbers 14:28-33; Psalm 95:8-11

19. Numbers 11

20. Exodus 32

21. Numbers 25:1-3

22. Numbers 21:4-5

23. Numbers 13:31ff

24. Numbers 14:1-14

25. Numbers 16:41

26. Edwards, 249.

CHAPTER 12

Fleeing Contact with Idols

1 Corinthians 10:14-11:1

Therefore, my dear friends, flee from idolatry. I speak to sensible people; judge for yourselves what I say. Is not the cup of thanksgiving for which we give thanks a participation in the blood of Christ? And is not the bread that we break a participation in the body of Christ? Because there is one loaf, we, who are many, are one body, for we all partake of the one loaf.

Consider the people of Israel: Do not those who eat the sacrifices participate in the altar? Do I mean then that a sacrifice offered to an idol is anything, or that an idol is anything? No, but the sacrifices of pagans are offered to demons, not to God, and I do not want you to be participants with demons. You cannot drink the cup of the Lord and the cup of demons too; you cannot have a part in both the Lord's table and the table of demons. Are we trying to arouse the Lord's jealousy? Are we stronger than he?

"Everything is permissible"—but not everything is beneficial. "Everything is permissible"—but not everything is constructive. Nobody should seek his own good, but the good of others.

Eat anything sold in the meat market without raising questions of conscience, for, "The earth is the Lord's, and everything in it."

If some unbeliever invites you to a meal and you want to go, eat whatever is put before you without raising questions of conscience. But if anyone says to you, "This has been offered in sacrifice," then do not eat it, both for the sake of the man who told you and for conscience' sake—the other man's conscience, I mean, not yours. For why should my freedom be judged by another's conscience? If I take part in the meal with thankfulness, why am I denounced because of something I thank God for?

So whether you eat or drink or whatever you do, do it all for the glory of God. Do not cause anyone to stumble, whether Jews, Greeks or the church of God—even as I try to please everybody in every way. For I am not seeking my own good but the good of many, so that they may be saved. Follow my example, as I follow the example of Christ.

A nobleman wanted to hire a driver for his horse-drawn carriage to take him over a dangerous mountain pass. Pointing to the edge of the road that dropped off into a steep cliff, the nobleman, appearing to test their skill, asked each prospective driver, "How close can you come to the edge of the cliff without going over?" One by one the hopefuls described how close they could come. Finally one fellow replied, "Sir, I'd stay as far away from that cliff as possible." Needless to say, he got the job!

It is Paul's desire in our text to persuade the Corinthians to stay as far away from idolatry as possible. He has just demonstrated the awful results of the worship of idols in Israel's history. With all their spiritual privilege and supernatural provision, they turned from the one true God, who delivered them from Egypt, to the gods of the heathen, and brought upon themselves severe judgment.

Paul fears that the "strong" Corinthian believers will fail to learn from Israel's example and will yield to the temptation to idolatry originating in continuing contact with idol temples and the eating of idol food. He pleads with them,

"Therefore, my dear friends, flee[2] from idolatry" (10:14). Although his warning was sharp and unmistakably connected to their behavior, his words, "my dear friends," (literally "my beloved ones") demonstrate exactly how much he cares for this church.

Idolatry Is Incompatible with Christian Communion (10:14-18)

Appealing to their common sense[3] (10:15), Paul explains why it is inconceivable that they could participate in both the Christian sacrament of the Lord's Supper and any similar idolatrous rite involving eating sacrificial food. He describes the elements of their Communion Table as "the cup of thanksgiving [blessing] for which we give thanks" (i.e., over which we say the blessing); and "the bread that we break" (10:16). The phrase "cup of blessing" was a technical Jewish term for the cup of wine drunk at the end of a meal as its formal close. Grace was said over it: "Blessed art thou, O Lord our God, who givest us the fruit of the vine." In the Passover meal, this cup was the third of four that had to be drunk, and was likely the cup about which Jesus said, "This cup is the new covenant in my blood."

Paul reminds the Corinthians that drinking the cup and eating the broken bread is a "participation" (sharing; communion)[4] in Christ's blood and body. That is to say, those who receive these elements in faith are united to Christ and, by the Spirit, to one another. They partake of the benefits secured for them through the Savior's shed blood and broken body—benefits that include atonement for sin and justification through faith. Thus both "strong" and "weak" members need to remember that the body of Christ is not divided, but like the single loaf of which they all partake, they are one body united in the fellowship of Christ (10:17). They must, therefore, express this unity in their relationship to each other.

To illustrate the church's participation in the benefits of Christ's sacrifice, Paul turns to the sacrificial practices of national Israel. "Do not those who eat the sacrifices participate in the altar?" (10:18). Aaron and his sons were instructed:

> Take the grain offering left over from the offerings made to the LORD by fire and eat it prepared without yeast beside the altar, for it is most holy. . . . You and your sons and your daughters may eat the bread that was waved and the thigh that was presented. Eat them in a ceremonially clean place; they have been given to you and your children as your share of the Israelites' fellowship offerings.[5]

Not only the priests, but other Israelites participated in certain sacrificial meals. In the account of Saul's searching for his father's lost donkeys, his servant suggests that they seek the help of a "man of God" who was in the area. As they search, they meet some girls and ask them, "Is the seer here?" The young women reply:

> He's ahead of you. Hurry now; he has just come to our town today, for the people have a sacrifice at the high place. As soon as you enter the town, you will find him before he goes up to the high place to eat. The people will not begin eating until he comes, because he must bless the sacrifice; afterward, those who are invited will eat.[6]

Paul is saying that those who partook of these sacrificial meals participated in the spiritual benefits that the sacrifice made available. They were partners in the altar; and so, likewise, believers who partake of the Lord's Supper participate in Christ.

Idolatry Has Demonic Overtones (10:19-22)

At this point, the apostle returns to the specific problem he had enunciated in chapter 8.[7] Here, as there, he maintains that as far as true believers are concerned neither the sacri-

fice offered to an idol nor the idol itself have any real significance (10:19). He will not dispute that. But there is still a
risk in participating in a heathen sacrificial meal.[8] The danger is that the worship of idols possesses demonic overtones.
The powers of darkness are at work in idolatry. In the Song
of Moses, recorded in Deuteronomy 32, we are told:

> Jeshurun [that is Israel] grew fat and kicked; filled
> with food, he became heavy and sleek. He abandoned
> the God who made him and rejected the Rock his
> Savior. They made him jealous with their foreign
> gods and angered him with their detestable idols.
> *They sacrificed to demons*, [italics mine] which are not
> God—gods they had not known, gods that recently
> appeared, gods your father did not fear.[9]

The danger is not to be found in the piece of wood or
stone from which an idol is made, but in its being a tangible
expression of the demon behind it. It follows, therefore, that
"the sacrifices of pagans are offered to demons, not to God"
(10:20), and it behooves the Corinthian believers, strong or
weak, to avoid any possible connection with the "god of this
world" lest they "give the devil a foothold."[10]

Just as the Lord Jesus told His disciples, "No one can
serve two masters. Either he will hate the one and love the
other, or he will be devoted to the one and despise the
other,"[11] so Paul is warning the church in Corinth, "You
cannot drink the cup of the Lord and the cup of demons too;
you cannot have a part in both the Lord's table and the table
of demons" (10:21). A divided allegiance is impossible. To
attempt to have it both ways would result in "arous[ing] the
Lord's jealousy" (10:22), and insinuates that we "can play
fast and loose with our loyalty to him . . . and get away with
it."[12]

A missionary once told me of an African Christian who,
instead of destroying all the utensils connected with his former idolatry, kept some of them in his house, thinking that

they were perfectly innocent trinkets. As time went on, one bizarre phenomenon after another began to take place in his residence. Jars would fall from their shelves; family members would suddenly become ill with unexplainable symptoms; children would awaken at night, screaming with fear. Upon inquiring, the missionary discovered that the father had not destroyed every vestige of idolatry in the house and urged the African to sweep his place clean. The believer did as the missionary counseled, and as soon as he did so, the strange happenings ceased and peace reigned in the home.

Idolatry May Violate a Weak Conscience (10:23-30)

Paul now concludes his instruction concerning the eating of meat offered to idols. He counters the same popular slogan as he used in chapter 6, with regard to sexual immorality—"everything is permissible,"[13]—with the greater truths, "not everything is beneficial"[14]; and "not everything is constructive"[15] (10:23). Rather than selfishly seeking to satisfy one's own good, a believer should seek "the good of others" (10:24). This has the effect of building up the whole body.

Then, interestingly enough, he advises procedures which would require the weaker brother to accommodate himself to the stronger. First, "Eat anything sold in the meat market without raising questions of conscience, for, 'The earth is the Lord's, and everything in it' " (10:25-26). It was true that the meat sold in the shops might well have formed part of a sacrifice or have been slaughtered in the name of some god, but one can be too finicky and create difficulties where none need exist. And if, as Paul puts it, "I take part in the meal with thankfulness, why am I denounced because of something I thank God for?" (10:30). Following such advice might require a stretch for the weak brother, since he could not easily tell what had or had not been offered to idols. But where the well-being of the church is at stake, both weak and strong must make concessions to the other.

Second, when invited out for a meal, believers are free to eat whatever is placed before them "without raising questions of conscience" (10:27). The old expression, "What you don't know won't hurt you," seems to be appropriate in this case. So "Don't ask" is the advice Paul gives. If, however, the host specifically identifies the fare as idol-food, then for the sake of another man's conscience they should refrain from eating it (10:28). The assumption is that he is being told by one of the brothers whose conscience causes him to feel that eating such food is sinful.

Idolatry Does Not Glorify God (10:31-11:1)

Finally he lays down two great principles. First, whatever the strong Corinthian believers do, they are to be concerned for the glory of God. They must ask the question, "Does our contact with an idol temple, or our eating idol food, really contribute to the reputation of the only true God? Does our behavior cause His name to be praised and His majesty to be acknowledged in Corinth?" If it does not, then they must avoid these things altogether.

Second, they are to be concerned lest their contact with the idol temple cause anyone to stumble. Their concern must reach beyond the bounds of their Christian fellowship to include all men, whether from the Jewish or pagan communities. In this they are to follow Paul's example of putting the spiritual well-being of others before their own personal rights. This was the attitude of both Paul and his Lord whom he imitated.

Conclusion

Once again we observe how contemporary is the inspired Word of God. First of all, we need to be alert to the dangers of twentieth-century idolatry. While we do not bow down to idols of wood or stone, idolatry, for us, is holding anything, or anyone, in higher esteem than we hold our God and Savior. Paul, for example, classifies greed as idolatry.[16] We need to hear our Lord ask us the question He asked Peter, "Do you truly love me more than these?" And the only appropriate response is found in one stanza penned by Gerhard Ter-steegen, and translated by John Wesley:

> Is there a thing beneath the sun
> That strives with Thee my heart to share?
> Ah! tear it thence, and reign alone,
> The Lord of every motion there;
> Then shall my heart from earth be free,
> When it has found repose in Thee.[17]

Second, our text calls us to a greater understanding and appreciation of the Lord's Supper. When we gather around the Table to partake of the rich symbols of His body and blood, our text calls us to see afresh by faith our living union with Christ. This is a mystical union, made experientially real by the indwelling of the Spirit of Christ Himself. How precious, therefore, the Communion of the Lord's Supper becomes to those who partake of Christ. And how repulsive is anything that would entice us to a fellowship with demonic forces of darkness. Ours is a union with Christ, not with demons.

And third, our text calls us once again to surrender the right to follow our liberated conscience in matters not specifically forbidden by the Scripture if doing so would cause harm to a weaker brother or sister. This is an act of love. The beautiful Christological hymn of Philippians 2 sums it up:

> Each of you should look not only to your own interests, but also to the interests of others.
> Your attitude should be the same as that of Christ Jesus.
>
> Who, being in very nature God,
>   did not consider equality with God
>   something to be grasped,
>   but made himself nothing,
>   taking the very nature of a servant,

being made in human likeness.
And being found in appearance as a man,
  he humbled himself
  and became obedient to death—
    even death on a cross!
Therefore God exalted him to the highest place
  and gave him the name that is above every name,
that at the name of Jesus every knee should bow,
  in heaven and on earth and under the earth,
and every tongue confess that Jesus Christ is Lord,
  to the glory of God the Father.[18]

Endnotes

1. The Greek word *dioper*, translated here "therefore," is actually a stronger word than the one usually used. It is an argumentative conjunction indicating a very close logical conclusion with what has preceded it. It is used only here and in 8:13. Barrett, 230.

2. The verb is in the present imperative tense, indicating habitual practice; "keep on fleeing."

3. "I speak to *sensible people*"—He uses the adjective *phronimoi*, understanding." The word derives from *phrenes*, "diagphragm," early regarded as the seat of intellectual and spiritual activity. Here it means the power to judge. See Kittel, vol. IX, 221, 234.

4. *Koinonia*, meaning to share with someone in something. Kittel, vol. III, 804.

5. Leviticus 10:12-14

6. 1 Samuel 9:12-13

7. See chapter 9, "Giving Up One's Rights."

8. The "but" of 10:20, is the strong adversative *alla*.

9. Deuteronomy 32:15-17

10. Ephesians 4:27

11. Matthew 6:24

12. Barrett, 238.

13. See chapter 7.

14. The word is *sumpherei*—to help, be advantageous or profitable or useful or helpful.

15. Here the word is *oikodomei*—to benefit, strengthen, establish, edify.

16. Colossians 3:5

17. Taken from *The Church Hymnary* (London: Oxford University Press, n.d.), Hymn 459, "Thou Hidden Love of God."

18. Philippians 2:4-9

CHAPTER 13

Honoring the "Head"

1 Corinthians 11:2-16

I praise you for remembering me in everything and for holding to the teachings, just as I passed them on to you.

Now I want you to realize that the head of every man is Christ, and the head of the woman is man, and the head of Christ is God. Every man who prays or prophesies with his head covered dishonors his head. And every woman who prays or prophesies with her head uncovered dishonors her head—it is just as though her head were shaved. If a woman does not cover her head, she should have her hair cut off; and if it is a disgrace for a woman to have her hair cut or shaved off, she should cover her head. A man ought not to cover his head, since he is the image and glory of God; but the woman is the glory of man. For man did not come from woman, but woman from man; neither was man created for woman, but woman for man. For this reason, and because of the angels, the woman ought to have a sign of authority on her head.

In the Lord, however, woman is not independent of man, nor is man independent of woman. For as woman came from man, so also man is born of woman. But everything comes from God. Judge for yourselves: Is it proper for a woman to pray to God with her head uncovered? Does not the very nature of things teach you that if a man has

*long hair, it is a disgrace to him, but if a woman has long
hair, it is her glory? For long hair is given to her as a covering. If anyone wants to be contentious about this, we
have no other practice—nor do the churches of God.*

Considering the great variety of ethnic, religious, social and economic backgrounds represented in the
Corinthian church, it should not be surprising that
their worship services were fraught with problems of both
style and content. Jewish believers coming from a background of reserved and dignified synagogue services were
now worshiping with former idolaters whose pagan worship
styles had amounted to wild, orgiastic feasts where food and
wine were devoured in quantity. What style, then, was appropriate for the corporate worship of the God and Father of
Jesus Christ?

In Judaism, women played no major part in corporate
worship. They were restricted to certain sections of the
synagogue and were not permitted to read the lessons of the
service. Bringing these conservative traditions into the
Christian assembly would create considerable tension between Jewish members and the more permissive Greek believers, who were familiar with women priestesses, oracles
and temple attendants.

Paul is called upon to answer the Corinthian church's
questions concerning the character of their corporate worship services. In chapter 11, he gives guidelines concerning
the appropriate dress for men and women in church, specifically the covering of the head and instruction for the observance of the Lord's Supper. In chapters 12-14, he teaches the
assembly how to exercise Spirit-given ministries and manifestations in a loving and orderly manner.

These subjects sound fairly familiar to present-day evangelicals. Worship styles, the role of women, gifts of the
Spirit—each to some extent are a potential source of tension
in our assembly worship life, and each give opportunity for
saints with varying church backgrounds and personal tastes

to work out the "excellent way" of chapter 13 (love that never fails).

Several years ago our family lived next to a lady who showed interest in spiritual things and whom we desired to lead to the Lord. Her neighbors on the other side, recently moved in, were Christian people who invited her to attend special evangelistic services in their church. She attended, but the next day reported to my wife that she would never go there again. The speaker had made it clear that women should have hats on their heads in church and should never wear slacks, makeup or earrings because that is what the Bible taught. Since she was the only woman in the congregation without a hat, she felt that she had been singled out for ridicule. My wife sought to show her the difference between legalism and the love of Christ.

The preacher had based his remarks about wearing hats in church on the passage before us. But he had failed to separate what was peculiarly first-century Corinthian from the lasting principles that would be applicable to the church today. Granted, this is not easy, but if we would be sincere in applying the Scripture to life, we must try.

A Divinely Ordained Order (11:2-3)

Since he will have so much criticism of the church's behavior in the next few chapters, Paul begins with a word of praise for their holding to (so they thought!)[1] the teachings (likely the central truths of the Christian faith) which he had passed on to them (11:2).[2] But he plunges immediately into his intricate explanation of why, in public worship, men should not cover their heads and women should.

He begins his explanation (11:2-10) by setting forth a divinely instituted wise and universal order of headship (11:3).[3] God the Father, as Creator and Sustainer, is Head over all in the universe; Christ the Son, though He is one in essence with the Father, voluntarily and joyfully placed Himself under the Father's authority. He said, "I always do what pleases him."[4] Every Christian man is under the headship of Christ the Lord. The woman, though not at all inferior to the man any more than the Son is inferior to the Father, is under the headship of man.[5] She is called in the creation account a "helper suitable for him."[6]

The Divine Order Symbolized (11:4-5)

It is important that the Church, in her worship, recognize and symbolize this divinely instituted order of authority. In the Corinthian church, this would involve the appropriate use (for women) and non-use (for men) of a head covering. But some of both sexes were failing to exemplify this appropriate submission to their head. Some of the men had been worshiping with covered heads while some of the women had been praying or prophesying (11:5) with heads uncovered. The rather unstructured order of service would have made it possible for women to engage in this kind of ministry under the direct impulse of the Holy Spirit. But had Paul construed such a ministry to be a "teaching" or "leadership" ministry, he would not have permitted women to speak at all.[7]

Why might some men in the Corinthian church have been covering their heads in worship and some women not? A variety of possible answers have been given. As far as male worshipers were concerned, it might have been that Jewish men covered their heads in worship or that in the ancient world a cap was the sign of freedom.[8] As to the women, some suggest the possibility that well-to-do women in the church, especially those who had come from areas of the Mediterranean where head coverings were not considered necessary, thought the restriction of wearing a veil in public to be ridiculous.[9]

Others think that some Corinthian women were celebrating the truth that in Christ male and female distinctions were eradicated, and that by discarding their head coverings they were expressing their new existence as Christians.[10] Another answer is that the removal of the head covering represented part of a Gnostic tendency to play down the importance of the body.[11] Some authors see the tossing aside of the veil as a movement of Corinthian women toward independence.[12] Still others believe they were "simply following some of the more daring styles of the day."[13]

Imagine, however, how Jewish believers would have felt, coming from the conservative atmosphere of the synagogue. William Baird quips, "No doubt Cephas would have been shocked by such feminine exposure in the assembly, while Apollos might have considered it a matter of course."[14] Whatever their reasons, Paul seeks to persuade the Corinthian church to follow the usual custom of other churches (11:16).

The Symbolism Explained (11:4-10)

Paul explains the implications of the head covering for the Corinthian church. A man who covers his head in worship in the assembly would appear, in the eyes of Corinthian observers, to be dishonoring his "head," i.e., Christ (11:4), since he would be obscuring God's image and diminishing His glory (11:7). For a woman to uncover her head in the church would be to dishonor her "head," i.e., the man (11:5), since, among other things, she would appear to be acknowledging no visible authority (11:10)[15] and obliterating the creation distinction between male and female.[16]

Furthermore, her bare head might prove a source of embarrassment to her husband[17] and a temptation for other men to lust[18] since, according to some scholars, the unveiled head was a sign of a prostitute or a paid entertainer.[19]

A Divinely Ordained Interdependence (11:11-12)

At this point, Paul, not wanting to relegate women to a place of inferiority to men, acknowledges the God-ordained mutual interdependency of men and women (11:11-12). In the creation account, Adam was created directly by the hand of God from the dust of the earth, while Eve was taken from Adam's rib. But ever since, man has been "born of woman"

(11:12) and cannot exist without her. In the final analysis, both male and female are completely dependent upon God, the source of everything.

The close relationship between man and woman is accentuated all the more "in the Lord" (11:11). Paul tells the Galatians, "You are all sons of God through faith in Christ Jesus, for all of you who were baptized into Christ have clothed yourselves with Christ. There is neither Jew nor Greek, slave nor free, male nor female, for you are all one in Christ Jesus."[20] It would not be right, however, to say that by this statement the order of authority is obliterated. Paul is speaking about the union of believers with the Lord Jesus—a union that knows no ethnic, social nor sexual distinctions.

Finally, Paul calls upon his readers as Christian people to use common sense (11:13) and recognize that even nature makes gender distinctions that need to be recognized in public worship (11:14-15). But Paul has no intention of arguing the matter further with anyone who is given to "wordy battles." He ends the section by appealing to what is customary in all the other churches he has founded (11:16).

Conclusion

What are some particular lessons that we may learn and apply from this passage so full of "local color"? Certainly we would want to avoid anything that would bring reproach upon our families or upon the gospel of Christ. We would not wish to destroy symbolic gender distinctions, nor render void the God-ordained principle of mutual submission one to another. We would want to respect generally received church custom and do our best to avoid causing anyone to stumble. We would not wish to use the assembly of the saints as a place for showing off fashions or wearing anything that would distract people from the pure worship of God.

It should be clear that what was important in the Corinthian situation as far as Paul was concerned and what is vital for us today is our inner attitudes.[21] The inappropriate actions which men and women of that church were taking with respect to head coverings was but an expression of a lack of reverence toward God, a failure to respect God-ordained authority and a failure to honor one another.

Similar inward attitudes in our assemblies today may issue in outward symptoms, equally distressing to the angels (11:10),[22] such as immodest apparel (hats have lost their spiritual significance), defiant postures, arrogant gestures or even seating arrangements that signify disinterest or rebellion or desire to avoid certain members. The quest by some very gifted women for ministry not accorded them by Scripture speaks of the same disrespect for the God-ordained order.[23] The Church needs to be careful that she does not allow the spirit of the age to influence her thought away from the will of God revealed in Scripture.

The God-ordained order, if followed, would make for peace, social stability and strong family life and would bring God's blessing upon His Church.

Endnotes

1. Barrett, p. 247, implies this.

2. The word translated "teaching" is *paradosis*, meaning "tradition," i.e., truth, that has been passed down from a particular source. Jesus condemned the "tradition" that had been initiated by the elders since it did not find its source in God. Paul would have agreed with Jesus on that point. But he is speaking here about truth that initiated with Jesus—gospel truth which in Paul's time was still being passed down orally from evangelist to teacher to convert and was in the process of acquiring a fixed verbal form. See Kittel, vol. II, 172.

3. There has been a good deal of discussion as to whether Paul uses "head" to mean "source" or "authority." While there may be a few instances where "source" is its meaning, the overwhelming evidence seems to be that "head" usually means authority, as it does in this verse. This is the interpretation of Calvin, p. 353-354; Dods, p. 249;

Grosheide, p. 249; and more recently, evangelical scholar Wayne Gruden who makes his case in the text he edited with John Piper, *Recovering Biblical Manhood and Womanhood* (Wheaton, IL: Crossway Books, 1991), Appendix 1: "The Meaning of *Kephale*," 425ff.

4. See John 8:29

5. This certainly does not mean that a woman cannot come directly to her heavenly Father through His Son the Lord Jesus just as a man does. She does not need any other priest than our Great High Priest, Jesus Himself. Nor is there any license given to men to sexually, emotionally or physically abuse women. The Scripture nowhere countenances such behavior. Husbands, for example, are to "love [their] wives, just as Christ loved the church" (Ephesians 5:25). We are all to "love our neighbor" as ourselves. Men *and* women are neighbors!

6. Genesis 2:18

7. See 1 Corinthians 14: 33-35 and chapter 19 of this commentary.

8. See Barrett, 250.

9. See Craig S. Keener, *Paul, Women and Wives* (Peabody, MA: Hendrickson Publishers, 1992), 30.

10. See Brendan Byrne, *Paul and the Christian Woman* (Collegeville, MN: The Liturgical Press, 1988), 49; and also J. Stanley Glen, 129.

11. Ibid, 49ff.

12. See Marcus Dods, 248.

13. See William Baird, *The Corinthian Church—A Biblical Approach to Urban Culture* (Nashville, TN: Abingdon Press, 1964), 122. Baird states that "most Greek women had abandoned the veil, and were experimenting with countless styles of coiffure."

14. p. 122.

15. Marcus Dods, 250.

16. Barrett, 251; also Byrne, 49ff.

17. See Keener, 36. He adds, "The point of Paul's opening arguments about the head . . . calls us as believers to give up personal rights for the sake of honoring our families. . . . If dressing a certain way in public will cause discomfort to our spouse, we ought not to do it. . . ."

18. Ibid., 30. He suggests that for some observers in the assembly, the women's uncovered heads might connote "an invitation to lust. The issue in the Corinthian church may thus have been a clash of cultural values concerning modesty, and Paul wants the more liberated elements within the church to care enough about their more conservative colleagues not to offend them in this dramatic way."

19. But others like Fee, p. 511, see "no contemporary evidence" to support this view. W.G. Kummel, quoted in Baird, p. 122, "argues that the interpretation of the unveiled head as a sign of prostitution is not correct, since Greek women in this period could wear the veil or not depending on shifting styles."

20. Galatians 3:26-28

21. It needs to be said, however, that what is right because it is fixed in the creative relationship of men to women is not a matter of attitude but of divine intent. What is cultural can be remedied attitudinally if necessary.

22. The expression "because of the angels" (11:10) is interpreted as meaning (1) the holy angels who observe Christian worship would be distressed by the variation of the created order set out in verse 3, represented by the uncovered heads of women; (2) fallen angels (as in Genesis 6) might lust after the Corinthian women. I believe this idea is rightly, rejected by Barrett, p. 253, and by Morris, p. 154.

23. The statement is sometimes made that since some women seem gifted for pastoral leadership, therefore the

Lord must want them to be pastors. The question is not, What do they seem gifted for? but rather, What is the will of God defined in Scripture? See 10:32.

CHAPTER 14

Celebrating Communion

1 Corinthians 11:17-34

In the following directives I have no praise for you, for your meetings do more harm than good. In the first place, I hear that when you come together as a church, there are divisions among you, and to some extent I believe it. No doubt there have to be differences among you to show which of you have God's approval. When you come together, it is not the Lord's Supper you eat, for as you eat, each of you goes ahead without waiting for anybody else. One remains hungry, another gets drunk. Don't you have homes to eat and drink in? Or do you despise the church of God and humiliate those who have nothing? What shall I say to you? Shall I praise you for this? Certainly not!

For I received from the Lord what I also passed on to you: The Lord Jesus, on the night he was betrayed, took bread, and when he had given thanks, he broke it and said, "This is my body, which is for you; do this in remembrance of me." In the same way, after supper he took the cup, saying, "This cup is the new covenant in my blood; do this, whenever you drink it, in remembrance of me." For whenever you eat this bread and drink this cup, you proclaim the Lord's death until he comes.

Therefore, whoever eats the bread or drinks the cup of the Lord in an unworthy manner will be guilty of sinning against the body and blood of the Lord. A man ought to examine himself before he eats of the bread and drinks of the cup. For anyone who eats and drinks without recognizing the body of the Lord eats and drinks judgment on himself. That is why many among you are weak and sick, and a number of you have fallen asleep. But if we judged ourselves, we would not come under judgment. When we are judged by the Lord, we are being disciplined so that we will not be condemned with the world.

So then, my brothers, when you come together to eat, wait for each other. If anyone is hungry, he should eat at home, so that when you meet together it may not result in judgment.

And when I come I will give further directions.

The same proud and unloving spirit that caused the Corinthian church to divide around their leaders (1 Corinthians 1-4), refused to discipline immorality (1 Corinthians 5) and resulted in unloving lawsuits (1 Corinthians 6) that caused strong brothers to ignore the feelings of the weak (1 Corinthians 8-10)—that same spirit manifested itself in what should have been the most powerful manifestation of Christian love, the Lord's Supper. Paul can hardly believe what is happening (11:18).

Honoring the Participants (11:17-22)

It seems that it was the custom of the early churches to come together not only for singing, prayer and instruction, but to eat a fellowship meal which came to be called the Love Feast, followed by the sacrament of the Lord's Table. Each family brought what it could to the Love Feast. Some brought much while others, like some slaves, brought very little, if anything. In an act of love, the food was pooled so that all had enough to eat without respect to what they contributed. The same spirit of love for the "body" that pervaded the Love Feast would then carry over into the observance of the Lord's Supper.[1]

But in the assembly of God in Corinth, what should have been an occasion for beautiful fellowship had been turned into an episode of ugliness; what should have fostered the edification of all, humiliated many (11:22). Noticeably absent from the supper were ordinary politeness (11:21a), sharing (11:21b) and concern for the well-being of others (11:22). Present were selfish cliquishness (11:18), thoughtless gorging and drunkenness (11:21) and a failure to distinguish this kind of ravenous feasting from the sacrament of holy Communion.

As far as Paul was concerned, the kind of selfish spirit that pervaded these unloving feasts made a genuinely Christian partaking of the Lord's Supper impossible (11:20). For if the love of Christ were absent from the Love Feast, it would have been absent from the Lord's Table as well, and this would have resulted in their eating and drinking in an unworthy manner (11:27). Surely the sumptuous gratification of hunger and thirst should have been restricted to the privacy of their own homes (11:22).[2]

Remembering the Savior (11:23-26)

Paul now seeks to correct the Corinthians' degrading of the Communion service by setting before them its true meaning. There follow (11:23-26) those solemn and poignant words of explanation that most of us hear each time our churches gather around the Lord's Table.

This, says Paul, is a very special supper, first, because of *its historical roots* (11:23).[3] They take us back to the night of our Lord's betrayal by His own disciple, Judas Iscariot. He is eating His last Passover meal with the twelve in the upper room, commemorating Israel's protection from the angel of death through the sprinkled blood and their deliverance from Egyptian slavery.[4] After dismissing Judas, our Lord takes the cup and, it seems, almost casually changes the focus of the evening from the Passover to Himself. Paul is reminding his readers that the supper they were so terribly abusing was rooted in the very words and actions of their Lord on that dreadful night, and their observance of it must properly reflect the intense pathos of that event.

Second, the supper was very special because of its theological meaning (11:24-26). This is not just ordinary eating bread and drinking wine, but a partaking of elements that have immense spiritual significance. They symbolize the broken body and shed blood of Him whose death on the cross established a new covenant (agreement) between God and His people—a covenant which promises the forgiveness of every repentant believer's sins and a personal knowledge of and communion with Him (Jeremiah 31:31). The actual reception of these elements in faith signifies both a reappropriation of the saving gift of the gospel and a partaking of the saving life of Christ.[5]

Third, this Supper was special because of its confessional nature. The Lord's Table is a visual proclamation of the gospel (11:26). The entire rite, including the two elements themselves, the partaking of both and the perpetuation of the rite, powerfully portrays the good news that Christ's death was a sacrifice that made atonement for the sins of the world. It cries out that we are justified (forgiven and treated as though we had never sinned) freely through faith in the crucified Christ. And that there is coming a Day when Christ shall appear and we shall appear with him in glory, and the earthly Supper will no longer be necessary (11:26b). All of this is brought refreshingly to the minds and hearts of faithful communicants as they remember Jesus.

Ennobling the Supper (11:27-34)

Having set forth the meaning of the Supper, Paul defines the "worthy" manner in which it is to be received (11:27-34). He defines this as "recognizing the body of the Lord" (11:29). This means that those who partake of the supper must see beyond the physical nature of the bread and wine to what they represent—the broken body and shed blood of Christ poured out to reconcile sinners to God.

If, as some suggest, the "body of the Lord" here means the Church,[6] then to partake in a worthy manner means that the communicants would acknowledge that at the Lord's Table gender, ethnic, social and economic distinctions fade away, and all are one in the love of Christ.[7]

Partaking in a worthy manner necessitates self-examination (11:28) if one wishes to avoid the judgment of God. I remember how anxious I became when I read the King James version of this passage. Verse 29 reads, "For he that eateth and drinketh unworthily, eateth and drinketh damnation to himself, not discerning the Lord's body." I sought during each communion service, through an almost morbid self-examination, to find some worthiness in myself that would enable me to escape "damnation." I was never quite sure that I should be taking the bread and the cup "worthily." Unfortunately there are still some people in our churches who never take Communion because they never feel they are deserving!

I remember the relief that came to me when it dawned on my unworthy soul that personal worthiness was not the issue here. This was not a table for worthy people, but for repentant sinners saved by grace. The more keenly one felt his sinfulness, the more one needed the table. It was the table at which the "Friend of sinners" was the host, and I knew that I qualified to be His friend! This revelation to my heart, together with a better exegesis of the passage, made the celebration of Communion a wonderful occasion where I found fresh mercy and acceptance by God.

Self-examination in this context means making sure that I understand the meaning of the table, that I recognize the Lord's body and that I come honestly before God, "just as I am without one plea, but that [Christ's] blood was shed for me." This sort of judging ourselves is what Paul is talking about here—an exercise that ensures eating and drinking in a worthy manner and thus precludes God's disciplining judgments (11:29-32).[8]

Conclusion

After I had been John's pastor for a year or so, I wondered why he left the church during the hymn just before the Communion service. When I asked him why, he confided in me that he didn't feel worthy to partake. "Is there some sin in your life you are unwilling to let go?" I asked. He did not know of any. He just felt that he was not spiritual enough to partake of the Lord's Supper. I could identify with him, for I had felt the same unworthiness.

What believers like John need to understand is that appropriate preparation for Communion entails neither an inward recital of one's own righteousness nor a morbid introspection that tries to discover sins and failures that may not be there. Proper preparation involves not only understanding the meaning of the Supper but also a free and full confession of whatever sin the Holy Spirit convicts us. This enables us to partake with a cleansed conscience, unafraid, because we have judged ourselves, removing the necessity of God's judging us. It may also be necessary, in fully purifying the conscience, to make things right with a brother or sister.[9]

The devil nags our consciences, never pinpointing exactly what is wrong and never reminding us that there is mercy with the Lord. The Holy Spirit, however, is specific about what needs to be confessed and always reminds us that "If we confess our sins, [God] is faithful and just and will forgive us our sins and purify us from all unrighteousness."[10]

Joseph Hart's hymn, "Come, Ye Sinners, Poor and Needy," can be a very appropriate invitation to the Lord's Table:

> Come, ye sinners, poor and needy,
> Weak and wounded, sick and sore;
> Jesus ready stands to save you,
> Full of pity, love and power:
> He is able; He is willing; doubt no more!
> Now, ye needy, come and welcome;

God's free bounty glorify:
True belief and true repentance—
Every grace that brings you nigh—
Without money, come to Jesus Christ and buy.

Come, ye weary, heavy laden,
Bruised and ruined by the fall;
If you tarry till you're better,
You will never come at all:
Not the righteous,
Sinners Jesus came to call.

Let not conscience make you linger,
Nor of fitness fondly dream;
All the fitness He requireth
Is to feel your need of Him:
This He gives you—
'Tis the Spirit's rising beam.

Lo, th' incarnate God ascended,
Pleads the merit of His blood;
Venture on Him, venture wholly,
Let no other trust intrude;
None but Jesus
Can do helpless sinners good.[11]

Endnotes

1. Morris, 158.
2. At one time in some evangelical churches the question, "Don't you have homes to eat and drink in?" meant that suppers should not be held in the church building. I remember the tension that developed in one church when, during the weekend when their new building was to be dedicated, a church supper was held in the basement! Many came to the supper; others stayed away and missed a time of rich blessing and fellowship. Paul is not

so much objecting to where the meal is being eaten as to the way in which the participants are behaving.

3. The emphatic *ego* ("I") at the beginning of 11:23, might indicate that Paul received the tradition of the Communion directly from the Lord Jesus Himself rather than from other apostles.

4. Exodus 12:1-30. The Passover itself is a beautiful picture of redemption from bondage to sin, through Christ's blood, "sprinkled" by faith on the heart of a believer.

5. In John 6:53-58, Jesus speaks about eating His flesh and drinking His blood. He says, "The one who feeds on me will live because of me." There is clearly a Communion motif in this passage. Partaking of the bread and wine is not only a way of remembering the death of Christ, but it is also a way of symbolizing the believer's reception of the saving life of Christ (eternal life) into his or her soul.

6. See for instance, Baird, p. 136 and Moffatt, p. 171. Cf. 10:17.

7. This is of course true, regardless of the particular meaning of "body" at this point.

8. Commenting on the phrase, "and a number of you have fallen asleep" (11:30), Canon H.L. Goudge, *The First Epistle to the Corinthians* (London: Methuen & Co. Ltd., 1926), 102, states: "The severity of God's judgments upon sin in the Apostolic Church was the necessary result of the closeness of His union with her. Sin is more (or less) sinful according to the clearness of our recognition of the will of God, and the closeness of our union with Him. When the Church has become mingled with the world, both the blessing and the responsibility of belonging to her fellowship are diminished."

9. See our Lord's words in Matthew 5:23-24.

10. 1 John 1:9

11. *Hymns of the Christian Life* (Harrisburg, PA: Christian Publications, 1978), number 555.

CHAPTER 15

Enabling Spiritual Ministry

1 Corinthians 12:1-11

Now about spiritual gifts, brothers, I do not want you to be ignorant. You know that when you were pagans, somehow or other you were influenced and led astray to mute idols. Therefore I tell you that no one who is speaking by the Spirit of God says, "Jesus be cursed," and no one can say, "Jesus is Lord," except by the Holy Spirit.

There are different kinds of gifts, but the same Spirit. There are different kinds of service, but the same Lord. There are different kinds of working, but the same God works all of them in all men.

Now to each one the manifestation of the Spirit is given for the common good. To one there is given through the Spirit the message of wisdom, to another the message of knowledge by means of the same Spirit, to another faith by the same Spirit, to another gifts of healing by that one Spirit, to another miraculous powers, to another prophecy, to another distinguishing between spirits, to another speaking in different kinds of tongues, and to still another the interpretation of tongues. All these are the work of one and the same Spirit, and he gives them to each one, just as he determines.

Y ou will recall that at the very beginning of his letter to the Corinthians the Apostle Paul thanks God that this church did "not lack any spiritual gift" (1:7). This was no stagnant congregation. With all their problems, they were very much alive in the Spirit. What they did evidently lack, however, was the awareness of how to exercise their spiritual gifts in an appropriate and loving manner. Although there was manifested among them a full range of the *gifts* of the Spirit, a simultaneous expression of the *fruit* of the Spirit (love) was lacking.

This lack of love was evident in the litigious spirit among them (6:1-11); in the disregard of the "weak" by the "strong" (chapter 8); in the abuse of the Love Feast and Communion (11:17ff); in the apparent arrogance of those who considered their giftedness to be superior to that of others (12:21f); in the feelings of inferiority in those who felt their gifts to be of minor significance in the body (12:14ff); and in the disorderly confusion of their worship services, in which it seems the Corinthians abused the gifts of the Spirit for ostentation and show (11:17-34 and chapter 14).

As we know, Paul had become aware of all these exhibitions of the flesh either through the letter he had received from them (7:1) or through the oral report brought by members of Chloe's household (1:11). In chapters 12-14, he continues his corrective ministry, instructing his readers concerning the content of a truly Christian confession of faith (12:1-3), the diversity of spiritual gifts (12:4-11), the significance of each person's gift in the assembly (12:12-31) and the vital requirement that gifts be exercised in a loving and orderly fashion (chapters 13-14).

The Spirit's Presence Verified (12:1-3)

In an assembly such as Corinth's where powerful supernatural manifestations are present, it is important to distinguish those that find their source in the Spirit of God from those that don't. Apparently (though it is difficult for us to imagine) there were occasions in the Corinthian assembly when someone under the influence of what he thought to be the Holy Spirit would actually utter the words, "Jesus be cursed."[1]

Paul attributes such a blasphemous confession to the influence of demonic forces that seized hold of pagan idol worshipers in the exercise of their ecstatic cults (12:2). In no way would the Holy Spirit elicit such a confession. Rather, the Spirit prompts and enables the person He is influencing to confess, "Jesus is Lord" (12:3). This was the powerful saving confession made by believers at their baptism that could ultimately lead to the martyrdom of those who made it. It would, therefore, not likely be made thoughtlessly, insincerely or hypocritically.

Today, perhaps as never before, we must take heed to the admonition of the Apostle John in his first letter, warning his readers not to gullibly believe every manifestation or thought that purports to come from the Holy Spirit. He instructs us to "test the spirits,"[2] in order to separate the false from the true. And the supreme test of the validity of a spiritual confession or the soundness of a body of doctrine is that it affirms the divinity and Lordship of Jesus Christ as He is presented to us in the Gospels. Of the Holy Spirit, Jesus Himself said to His disciples, "He will bring glory to me by taking from what is mine and making it known to you."[3] It is vital that we assert as never before the absolute centrality of Jesus Christ, crucified, buried and risen from the dead.

The Spirit's Manifestations Categorized (12:4-6)

Paul now describes the manifestations of the Spirit in terms of their *nature* and of their *source*. In describing their nature, Paul uses three important words. He calls them first "gifts" (12:4). The Greek word is *charismata*, which emphasizes the truth that all these manifestations are given to the Church freely as an expression of God's grace. Just as the Father gave to the world the free gift of His Son and the Son gave to the Church the free gift of the Spirit, so the Spirit gives to the individual members gifts that are neither earned, merited or the marks of spiritual maturity. It is important that the members recognize this in order that they not become proud of their individual contributions.

During a revival in our church, several of our people were given rather spectacular manifestations of the Spirit, including the gift of tongues. One young couple who received this gift became convinced that it indicated a maturity considerably beyond the "common folk" in our congregation, and they began to not so subtly insinuate that they were spiritually superior. This eventually called for gentle but firm confrontation by our elders, who assured them that this gift was no sign of maturity and that if they loved their brothers and sisters in the assembly, they would change their attitudes. Fortunately the young couple was mature enough to respond positively to the el-ders' reproof.

Second, Paul calls these manifestations kinds of "service" (12:5). The word is *diakonia*, a term suggesting that the purpose of the gifts is for loving ministry within the body. They are not given for selfish aggrandizement but because the Head of the Church desires that its members should "serve one another in love."[4] Just as Christ came not to be served, but to serve in the power of the Holy Spirit who anointed Him, so it is His will that believers, through the exercise of gifts of the Spirit, should demonstrate the same servant spirit that characterized their Lord.

Third, Paul speaks of there being different kinds of "working," *energemata* (12:6). This word suggests that in all these manifestations, God is powerfully at work by His Spirit. Something good is really happening that will help, heal, encourage or strengthen other believers.

The source of these manifestations is in the Triune God. There may be different kinds (literally "distributions") of manifestations, allotted sovereignly to different believers, but each and all spring from the Father, Son and Holy Spirit. As one author so beautifully puts it, "The variety of the Spirit's operations is the variety not of division but of unity. The diversity is corporate not competitive; the variety is . . . [like] the multicolored rays that stream from the noon sun, all centered in One Orb because all emanate from the One Orb. . . ."[5]

The Spirit's Gifts Specified (12:7-11)

There follows a catalog of nine manifestations of the Spirit given to individual members (12:7) at the sovereign discretion of the Holy Spirit (12:11) for the good of the whole assembly (12:7). Each is beyond and independent of any knowledge or ability that a person can have without them. They are commonly grouped into three classifications: gifts of revelation (wisdom, knowledge and discerning of spirits), power (faith, miracles and healing) and inspiration (prophecy, tongues and interpretation of tongues).[6] Let us view them in the order in which Paul gives them:

1. "The message (word) of wisdom" (12:8a) is a spoken word given to someone in a difficult situation which resolves the difficulty or silences an opponent.[7] Biblical examples of this gift are Solomon's famous solution to the problem of the living and dead babies;[8] Jesus' answer to His opponents' question, Is it right to pay taxes to Caesar?;[9] and the apostles' decision to appoint seven men to care for the Grecian widows.[10]

    I have seen it manifested quite unobtrusively on more than one occasion in elders' meetings, annual meetings, general assemblies or counseling sessions.

2. "The message (word) of knowledge" (12:8b). A variety of meanings are suggested for this word. John Calvin thought it meant simply "acquaintance with sacred things."[11] Bittlinger suggests that it is "the old message spoken in the new situation in such a way that it still remains the old message." Commenting on John 14:26, he states, "Jesus gave His disciples the ability to speak the word of God with its unchanging sharpness into the contemporary situation."[12]

In more classic Pentecostal fashion, Horton defines the word of knowledge as "a divinely granted flash of revelation concerning things which were hopelessly hidden from the senses." He cites God's message of judgment for Eli, given as a voice in the night to the boy Samuel;[13] God's word to Ananias regarding the conversion of Saul of Tarsus;[14] and God's word to Peter regarding the arrival of messengers from Cornelius.[15]

Present-day illustrations of this gift of the Spirit could easily be cited. I am acquainted with several people who, in answer to prayer, were told by the Spirit where to look for something they had lost. Others have recounted how they were suddenly impressed to pray for some missionary or friend and discovered later how important that prayer was in bringing aid. I recall visiting a lady in the hospital whose doctors said they were unable to discover why she was not responding to treatment. As I stood beside her bed, the Holy Spirit prompted me to ask, "Would you tell me what terrible thing happened to you as a child?" Her immediate reply was, "Will God ever forgive for that?" We walked to the hospital chapel and knelt at the altar rail. Although I did not feel that what she had done needed forgiveness, she confessed what had happened and I assured her that her sin was forgiven. From that moment on, she began to recover.

3. "Faith" (12:9a). Paul is not referring to the faith necessary for salvation, but to what is commonly called, "mountain-moving faith." It is the conviction given to someone that God will assuredly reveal His power, righteousness and mercy in a specific case. He gave this gift to the Apostle Peter at the temple gate, Beautiful, enabling him to say, "In the name of Jesus Christ of Nazareth, walk."[16]

4. "Gifts of healing" (12:9b). This manifestation of the Spirit was continually evident in the ministry of our Lord Jesus to the diseased, lame, deaf and blind who

came to Him for help. It was continued in the ministry of the apostles[17] and has most surely not been removed from the life of the Church.

During his prayer on a Sunday morning, a pastor acquaintance of mine was interceding for a little child who was near death in the local hospital. He asked the compassionate Jesus to enter the boy's room and lay His healing hand upon the little one. As he prayed there came to his consciousness the complete assurance that the child was healed. News received following the service confirmed the answer to prayer. What a precious gift to the child, to the congregation and to the parents!

5. "Miraculous powers" (12:10a). A miracle is both a "wonder" and a "sign" calculated to produce a sense of awe in the beholders and to convey a message concerning the person or work of Christ, by whom or in whose name the miracle is performed. John tells us that the many recorded miracles of Jesus, such as turning water into wine at the marriage in Cana[18] and the feeding of the 5,000,[19] were recorded in order "that you may believe that Jesus is the Christ, the Son of God, and that by believing you may have life in His name."[20]

Reports from Africa tell us that on the frontiers of present-day evangelism, many of the unconverted have experienced miraculous healings and as a result have believed on the Lord Jesus, in whose name the signs and wonders were wrought.

6. "Prophecy" (12:10b). This is either a foretelling of the future or a forthtelling of the mind of God for a particular person or situation.[21] For example, after King David's affair with Bathsheba and his arranging the murder of her husband Uriah, God was displeased and sent the prophet Nathan to deliver a message. Hearing Nathan's story of the rich man who took the poor man's lamb, David became indignant and pronounced judgment on the rich man, to which Nathan replied, "You are the

man!" He then delivered a prophecy of judgment to the repentant king.[22]

7. "Distinguishing between spirits" (12:10c). The King James translation, "discerning of spirits," has been misinterpreted by some to mean the ability to know the inner mood, temper or motivation of another person. Perhaps a word of knowledge could reveal this. But the gift Paul is describing here means the ability to determine whether a supernatural manifestation has its source in the Spirit of God, a demonic spirit or the human spirit. The apostle manifested this gift when he exorcised the demonized slave girl who kept on shouting on the streets of Philippi, "These men are servants of the Most High God, who are telling you the way to be saved."[23]

This ability to distinguish between spirits is a necessary God-given protection for God's people from the intrusion of demonic activity into the assembly. On one occasion in the midst of revival, a stranger visited our church prayer meeting and began to pray in an unknown language. Instantly several of the members present discerned that this was not of the Holy Spirit, and the man was quietly asked to be still. He immediately left the meeting.

8. "Speaking in different kinds of tongues" (12:10d). This is supernatural utterance in a language that was never learned by the speaker. It may or may not be a language known to others. On the Day of Pentecost, the 120 disciples, filled with the Spirit, began to praise God in languages unknown to them but recognized by others who had come to the feast.[24]

9. "Interpretation of tongues" (12:10e) is not an exact translation of what is spoken, but a presentation in an understood language of the essential content of what was spoken in an unknown tongue.[25]

This list of the manifestations of the Spirit is probably not exhaustive but is rather representative of the many ways in which the risen Lord Jesus would desire to demonstrate His love and power among His Spirit-filled people gathered together.

Conclusion

The message of the "deeper life" offers us a Savior who, through the person of the Holy Spirit, is both an enablement to live a holy (Christlike) life and an enduement of power for witness to the world and ministry to the body of Christ. Both aspects of the deeper life need to be emphasized among God's people today. The late Paris Reidhead, former pastor of New York Gospel Tabernacle, used to say, "The gifts of the Spirit are hands and fingers by which love does its work." It is unfortunate that some branches of the evangelical church emphasize the gifts of the Spirit and neglect the fruit of the Spirit. This, as we have observed, was the problem in the church in Corinth.

But equally unfortunate is that other sections of evangelicalism emphasize the fruit of the Spirit (love) and ignore or disparage the manifestations of the Spirit set forth in our text. It was never Christ's intention that this either/or attitude should prevail toward the gifts and graces of the Spirit. The world needs to see how Christians "love one another," and it needs to be given opportunity to see manifested the mighty power of God. "Follow the way of love and eagerly desire spiritual gifts,"[26] was the word of the apostle to the Corinthians. Amen!

Endnotes

1. Commentators differ greatly in their explanations of how this could happen. Barrett, p. 280, offers five possibilities, none of which seems to me satisfactory. He tends to agree with Allo in the suggestion that "Paul is referring to the cries of Christian ecstatics who were resisting the trance or ecstasy they felt coming upon them." Arnold Bittlinger, *Gifts and Graces* (Grand Rapids,

MI: William B. Eerdman's Publishing Company, 1967), 17, offers the explanation that those who utter the words, "Jesus be accursed" are people who do not regard that expression and the expression "Jesus is Lord" to be contradictory. They are, thinks Bittlinger, people like some Gnostics who separate the historic Jesus from the spiritual Christ and who therefore can curse the human Jesus in the meeting for worship, believing they were speaking by the Spirit of God.

2. 1 John 4:1ff. John is not only referring to the kind of testing of spirits that is sometimes done when demonization of an individual is suspected; he is primarily referring to the testing of the truth or falsehood of a teacher's doctrine concerning the nature of Jesus Christ. Gnostic thought which John is refuting in this letter taught that the man Jesus was not the Christ but that the Christ-Spirit came upon Him at His baptism and left Him at His death. John attributes that theology to the spirit of antichrist. The true Jesus, the Jesus whom the Holy Spirit exalts, is "Jesus Christ come in the flesh." The man Jesus is the Christ; they are one and the same.

3. John 16:14

4. Galatians 5:13

5. Harold Horton, *The Gifts of the Spirit* (Nottingham, England: Assemblies of God Publishing House, 1934), 29.

6. Horton, 33-34.

7. Bittlinger, p. 28. Horton, p. 67, defines it as the "supernatural revelation by the Spirit, of the Mind and Will of God; the supernatural unfolding of His plans and purposes concerning things, places, and people." Barrett, p. 284, finds it hard to distinguish between wisdom and knowledge and, rather weakly, defines the two together as the gift of instructive discourse.

8. 1 Kings 3:16-28

9. Luke 20:20-26

10. Acts 6:3
11. p. 401.
12. p. 30.
13. 1 Samuel 3:13
14. Acts 9:11-12
15. Acts 10:19
16. Acts 3:6
17. For instance, the healing of the cripple at Lystra (Acts 14:8-10).
18. John 2:1ff
19. John 6:1ff
20. John 20:31
21. The gift of prophecy will be treated in greater detail in chapter 13 of this commentary.
22. See 2 Samuel 12
23. Acts 16:16-18
24. Acts 2:4. The gift of tongues will be treated more fully in chapter 18.
25. See also chapter 18 of this commentary.
26. 1 Corinthians 14:1

CHAPTER 16

Unifying Spiritual Ministry

1 Corinthians 12:12-31

The body is a unit, though it is made up of many parts; and though all its parts are many, they form one body. So it is with Christ. For we were all baptized by one Spirit into one body—whether Jews or Greeks, slave or free— and we were all given the one Spirit to drink.

Now the body is not made up of one part but of many. If the foot should say, "Because I am not a hand, I do not belong to the body," it would not for that reason cease to be part of the body. And if the ear should say, "Because I am not an eye, I do not belong to the body," it would not for that reason cease to be part of the body. If the whole body were an eye, where would the sense of hearing be? If the whole body were an ear, where would the sense of smell be? But in fact God has arranged the parts in the body, every one of them, just as he wanted them to be. If they were all one part, where would the body be? As it is, there are many parts, but one body.

The eye cannot say to the hand, "I don't need you!" And the head cannot say to the feet, "I don't need you!" On the contrary, those parts of the body that seem to be weaker are indispensable, and the parts that we think are less honorable we treat with special honor. And the parts that are unpresentable are treated with special modesty, while our presentable parts need no special treatment. But

God has combined the members of the body and has given greater honor to the parts that lacked it, so that there should be no division in the body, but that its parts should have equal concern for each other. If one part suffers, every part suffers with it; if one part is honored, every part rejoices with it.

Now you are the body of Christ, and each one of you is a part of it. And in the church God has appointed first of all apostles, second prophets, third teachers, then workers of miracles, also those having gifts of healing, those able to help others, those with gifts of administration, and those speaking in different kinds of tongues. Are all apostles? Are all prophets? Are all teachers? Do all work miracles? Do all have gifts of healing? Do all speak in tongues? Do all interpret? But eagerly desire the greater gifts.

And now I will show you the most excellent way.

Having set before the Corinthian believers the great diversity of ministries in the Church, each contributing to the "common good" (12:7), Paul now teaches them that the diverse ministries function together in the one Body of Christ, the Church—diversity in unity.

A Spirit-Constituted Body (12:12-13)

Paul likens the operation of ministry within the Church to the constitution and functioning of the human body (12:12). When I look at you, I do not see you as a head, arms, hands, legs, eyes, nose, stomach, lungs, heart, liver and whatever other parts your body has. When everything is operating normally, I see you as one whole wonderful body. I would likely only notice your arm if it were in a sling. I know that you possess all those parts; some are visible, others hidden. I know that each is necessary for the robust functioning of your body. I know too that no one part of your body is the whole. I am amazed at the order and beauty of God's creation in you.

This, says Paul, is an illustration of how it is in the local body of Christ. Whatever our ethnic backgrounds (Jews or

Greeks) or social status (slave or free), the Holy Spirit has joined us all together as a living organism—the body of Christ (12:13-14); and He, the Living Water, the Thirst Quencher, now dwells within us, "a spring of water welling up to eternal life."[1] As Jesus had promised, speaking of the Spirit, "Whoever believes in me, as the Scripture has said, streams of living water will flow from within him."[2]

Spirit-Dispensed Equality (12:14-27)

When it comes to ministry within the Body, there is no need for a sense of inferiority or dissatisfaction. Referring again to the human body, Paul imagines a foot feeling left out because it is not a hand (12:15) or an ear feeling frustrated because it is not an eye (12:16). Each member's function, whatever its nature, is necessary for the healthy operation of the whole. What a bizarre creature you would have if a human being were just a large eye or a monstrous ear (12:17)—if only one of the five senses were operating. This would be a distortion of what our Creator God had designed (12:18-19). There would be no body!

Paul intends us to see immediately how absurd it would be for any believer to think that because he does not have another's giftedness he is therefore worthless in the life of the Church. It is the Holy Spirit who graciously distributes His gifts within the Body of Christ, not as we determine but as He determines (12:11). There is no useless function, and to disparage our gift is to belittle the One who gave it. Writing to the church at Rome, the apostle declares:

> We have different gifts, according to the grace given us. If a man's gift is prophesying, let him use it in proportion to his faith. If it is serving, let him serve; if it is teaching, let him teach; if it is encouraging, let him encourage; if it is contributing to the needs of others, let him give generously; if it is leadership, let him govern diligently; if it is showing mercy, let him do it cheerfully.[3]

For several months, I taught a class in Bible doctrine in the lower auditorium of our church. Each evening about an hour before the class began, an elderly gentleman came downstairs and carefully arranged the seating just the way he knew I liked it. He made sure the overhead projector was in exactly the right position, placed a glass of water on the desk behind which I would stand and picked up the debris from the previous night's session. I could not have taught nearly so efficiently had he not served so faithfully. His ministry and mine were quite different, but we complemented each other perfectly. How foolish it would have been had he said, "Because I cannot teach, I will not serve."

Neither is there room in the ministry of the body for feelings of superiority. Imagine an eye not needing a hand! What good is an eye if it cannot perform its task? Imagine a head (the highest part) not needing feet (the lowest). What good is a head if it cannot go anywhere? Arnold Bittlinger quotes this parable from the ancient writer, Livy:

> There was a day when the human body was not as harmoniously ordered as it is today. Every member of the body had its own will and its own language. The other members became angry that they had to concern themselves with the need of the stomach and provide it with everything. The stomach just remained at the center of all this, satisfied with all that was brought to it. The members made this decision: the hands would not supply any food to the mouth— the mouth would not receive any food nor would the teeth chew. Consequently during this time in which they starved the stomach all the parts of the body became weak and feeble. Then they realized that the role of the stomach was not to be despised as a passive one. Just as he was being nourished, he was passing on strength in return.[4]

In our text, Paul tells us that there are no indispensable members in the Body of Christ; we *need* each other (12:21).

I recall a young man in our congregation who believed that the Holy Spirit had given him the gift of prophecy. Compared with other members of our congregation, he was quite immature, but he began to let it be known in attitude and word that possession of this gift made him distinctly superior to the rest of the flock. He could function quite nicely, thank you, without the help of ordinary souls. It appeared he did have a prophetic gift, but he used it in unwise ways, and his attitude was repugnant to the rest of God's people, some of whom described his gift as "divisive." The pastor who sought to teach the people that it was not the gift, but his attitude that was divisive, gently confronted the young man, who repented of his pride, publicly acknowledged his sin against the church and began to learn that he needed the other members of the assembly as they needed him.

Not only must we recognize that we need each other, but we need learn to respect each other. Paul says, "the parts [of the body] that we think are less honorable we treat with special honor. And the parts that are unpresentable are treated with special modesty" (12:23).[5] Since God has given honor to "the parts that lacked it" (12:24b), members of the Body of Christ need to show honor to the seemingly most insignificant persons in their midst. We need to evaluate people not on the basis of what they do, but on the basis of who they are in Christ. Otherwise, we create divisions in the Body based on a false measure of people's worth.

Our text teaches that, as members of the Body of Christ, our lives are inextricably bound together. In the physical body, when a finger is hurt, the whole body feels the pain. In the Church when one member suffers, the whole assembly suffers (12:26a). Similarly, as there is a sense of national solidarity that causes an entire population to rejoice when a fellow citizen is honored, so in the Church, because it is bound together in a spiritual solidarity, when one member is honored, all the members rejoice with him (12:26b).

When one of our church members received his Ph.D. degree, it was announced to the congregation. There was an instant burst of applause and a sensation that the corporate assembly had earned a doctorate!

As if to clinch what he has been teaching the Corinthians, Paul states, "Now *you* are the body of Christ."[6] Therein lies its unity. "And each one of you is a part of it" (12:27). Therein exists its diversity. They must recognize that their diverse gifts of the Spirit are all given by Him for the upbuilding of the one Body. There is no room for a jealous or competitive spirit among them. Each is necessary for the fitting functioning of the whole.

Spirit-Appointed Offices (12:28-31)

Finally Paul lists some of the different offices that God has given for the governance and edification of the Church (12:28).

1. "Apostles"[7]—men originally chosen by Christ to be with Him and whom He sent out as initiate preachers and to cast out demons.[8] Later there appear to have been others than the twelve, like Barnabus, James and Paul, each of whom were highly esteemed as custodians of the gospel.

2. "Prophets"—persons enabled to speak words from God as revealed to them by the Holy Spirit, usually to local assemblies.

3. "Teachers"—mature believers who, gifted by the Spirit, instruct the Church in the meaning and implications of the Christian faith.[9]

4. "Workers of miracles"—those empowered by the Spirit to perform awe-inspiring deeds calculated to draw attention to the presence and power of the living Christ.

5. "Those having gifts of healing"[10]—the ability to bring health and wholeness to the sick and suffering.

6. "Those able to help others"—not an office, but the ability to lend support or help to those who need it.[11]

7. "Those with gifts of administration"—the ability to lead or direct the affairs of a congregation, to govern.[12]

8. "Those speaking in different kinds of tongues"—i.e., in languages they have not learned.[13]

Through a series of questions each demanding the answer "No," Paul makes clear that each of these offices does not belong to everyone (12:29-30), but that it would be appropriate to "eagerly desire the greater gifts" (12:31a). It appears that the Corinthians had been placing too high a value on the gift of speaking in tongues, and Paul is encouraging them to seek, by prayer and self-preparation, the gift of prophecy or of teaching, which would enable them to make a maximum contribution to the life of the church.[14] Whatever their gifts of the Spirit, the Corinthians must be sure that love, the fruit of the Spirit and the supreme mark of the Christian, thoroughly pervades all their ministry (12:31b).

Conclusion

One of the perils that must not only be avoided but striven against in a church is a competitive spirit that hinders healthy body life. The members of the Christ's body are not in competition with one another to gain prestige, position or power but are workers together for the well-being of the whole assembly. Believers who desire to walk in obedience to the Lord need to see themselves as Christ saw Himself—a humble love-slave. He said, "The greatest among you will be your servant."[15]

We must be willing to exercise our Spirit-given giftedness not to proudly draw attention to ourselves, but to humbly edify the whole body of believers. There is to be neither a spirit of jealousy over another's ability nor a spirit that "thinks more highly of itself than it ought," but rather a spirit that "thinks of itself with sober judgment in accordance with the measure of faith God has given."[16]

Loyalty to a local assembly is a trait in danger of being lost in today's consumer-oriented world, where the question is often, "What will this product or organization do for me and my family?" Unfortunately that spirit often motivates people in their relationship to a local church instead of a desire to contribute to the health and growth of the Body of Christ.

Let us "eagerly desire" to serve one another in love.

Endnotes

1. John 4:14

2. John 7:38

3. Romans 12:6-8

4. p. 54.

5. Commentators are not agreed as to what parts of the body are "weaker," "less honorable" or "unpresentable." But, nevertheless, the point is that great respect is given to the less honorable and unpresentable parts, probably by clothing them.

6. The wording of the Greek is especially significant—*humeis de este soma Christou.* "You" is first in the sentence, for emphasis, and "body" is without the definite article, pointing up the essential nature of the Corinthian church.

7. The noun *apostolos* (apostle) is derived from the verb *apostellein* (to send). Perhaps our word "missionary" would apply.

8. See Mark 3:14ff

9. In Ephesians 4:11 the Greek construction seems to connect the office of pastor to that of teacher—"pastor/teacher." This may indicate the primary, though not the only, task of a pastor.

10. The Greek *himation* is plural—"healings"—implying perhaps that each individual healing is a gift from the Spirit.

11. The word is *antilempseis*. A compound form of the corresponding verb *synantilambaneiv* (literally "to take hold on the other side with") is used in Romans 8:26 to describe the ministry of the Holy Spirit in "helping" us to pray in the will of God.

12. The word is *kubernesis* from a verb meaning "to steer a ship." Kittel, vol. III, speaks of this person as having the ability "to be a helmsman to his congregation, i.e., a true director of its order and therewith of its life."

13. See chapter 18 for a more detailed presentation of this gift.

14. Barrett, 296.

15. Matthew 23:11

16. Romans 12:3

CHAPTER 17

Preferring the Cardinal Virtue

1 Corinthians 13

If I speak in the tongues of men and of angels, but have not love, I am only a resounding gong or a clanging cymbal. If I have the gift of prophecy and can fathom all mysteries and all knowledge, and if I have a faith that can move mountains, but have not love, I am nothing. If I give all I possess to the poor and surrender my body to the flames, but have not love, I gain nothing.

Love is patient, love is kind. It does not envy, it does not boast, it is not proud. It is not rude, it is not self-seeking, it is not easily angered, it keeps no record of wrongs. Love does not delight in evil but rejoices with the truth. It always protects, always trusts, always hopes, always perseveres.

Love never fails. But where there are prophecies, they will cease; where there are tongues, they will be stilled; where there is knowledge, it will pass away. For we know in part and we prophesy in part, but when perfection comes, the imperfect disappears. When I was a child, I talked like a child, I thought like a child, I reasoned like a child. When I became a man, I put childish ways behind me. Now we see but a poor reflection as in a mirror; then we shall see face to face. Now I know in part; then I shall know fully, even as I am fully known.

And now these three remain: faith, hope and love. But the greatest of these is love.

We come to that most exquisite of Pauline passages, the beautiful "Hymn to Love" that celebrates what Henry Drummond called "the greatest thing in the world." The chapter's high literary excellence, the symmetry of its sentences and the grace and power of its vocabulary are seldom equaled by Paul. This has led some scholars to conclude that chapter 13, though composed by Paul, was not written exclusively for this letter but was inserted because he saw how relevant it was to the condition of the Corinthian church.[1]

Whether or not this was so, it is clear that "love" (*agape*) was the real remedy for the Corinthian ills. Division, incest, litigation, fornication, marital difficulty, disorder in worship—all would find their antidote in the command of the Lord Jesus to "Love each other as I have loved you."[2]

It would not be right, as some have done in their explanation of chapters 12 through 14, to set love against the manifestations of the Spirit as though there were a choice to be made between the two. During a period of fervent spiritual renewal in one local assembly, some of the more spectacular gifts of the Spirit were manifested. One believer, to whom such manifestations were new and somewhat feared, was heard to say, "They can have their gifts; give me love." This is a misunderstanding of God's intentions. True, the exercise of gifts without love can be unbecoming and in some cases repulsive. But it is just as true that without the exercise of the gifts of the Spirit, love is limited in its ability to minister to people's deepest needs. Someone has said that *mis*use is not corrected by *no* use, but by *right* use.

The Preeminence of Love (13:1-3)

Paul begins the chapter by insisting that even though one might speak in an unknown, even angelic tongue; prophesy; exercise mountain-moving faith; give generously to the poor;

or even die a martyr's death—if love were absent, the gifts would be of no profit.

During a series of revival meetings in our church, a charismatic minister came into the small prayer room following the evening service where people wanted to do business with God. He took a seat in the back row and, as soon as the people were settled in an attitude of prayer, began to pray loudly in an unknown tongue (13:1). This put a considerable damper on the prayer meeting. Up to that time, the people had never seen or heard anything like this in the long history of their church. The minister had manifested a gift of the Spirit in an unloving way.

The next night our friend returned and headed toward the prayer room. I took him aside before he could be seated, and quietly said to him, "My brother, you really love our people, don't you!" He replied, "Oh yes, I really do." "Then," I said, "if you really love these folk, you will pray in English tonight." Much to my delight, he replied, "You know, the Holy Spirit told me that before I came tonight." And he kept his word.

Paul notes that "faith" can be present without love (13:2). William Barclay tells of a man whose doctor told him that because of his physical condition, he must take time off from his work to rest. He went to his employer, a professing Christian, who listened to his need and then remarked, "I have an inward strength that enables me to carry on."[3] The not-so-subtle implication was, "I'm a better Christian than you." His was a faith that knew little love.

Furthermore, giving can be done without love (13:3). We remember the words of Jesus, "When you give to the needy, do not announce it with trumpets . . . but when you give to the needy, do not let your left hand know what your right hand is doing, so that your giving may be in secret. . . ."[4] He is warning His disciples against the danger of giving to enhance one's reputation.

Is it really possible that someone could court persecution out of impure motives? Might a person have such a sense of dedication to some high ideal that he will give himself to a death as painful as being consumed in flames, and do it without love (13:3b)? Evidently this is tragically possible. But as St. Augustine said, "It is not the death but the cause that makes a martyr."

The Portrait of Love (13:4-7)

Having set forth the preeminence of love, Paul fashions a beautiful fifteen-jeweled necklace, each gem of which describes what love looks or sounds like when one sees it, and together describe the fruit of the Holy Spirit reflected in the disposition of our Lord Jesus.

1. Love is patient (13:4). This fruit of the Spirit, which encompasses all the other fruit, describes patience with people, opposed to circumstances. In other passages, Paul encourages pastors to preach the word and to correct, rebuke and encourage with great patience.[5] He tells us how he ministered to the Corinthians in "patience and kindness."[6] Scripture describes God as being rich in patience[7] and encourages believers to be imitators of God[8] and to be patient with one another. Chrysostom said that "patience" is the word used of the man who is wronged and has it in his power to avenge himself yet will not.[9]

   If you have asked God for patience, you know how He usually answers that prayer—by bringing difficult people into our lives. The late Dr. Edman at Wheaton used to call such trying souls "God's sandpaper." Such folk teach us how little patience we have and encourage us to rely more heavily on the patient Holy Spirit.

2. Love is kind (13:4). Paul instructs the Thessalonians to "make sure that nobody pays back wrong for wrong, but always try to be kind to each other and to everyone else."[10] Kindness shows mercy and does works of love and compassion; kindness chooses its words carefully and does not make cutting remarks ("I just say what-

ever I think, and if the shoe fits, wear it!") or throw back cruel or retaliating words.

When I was young, my grandfather would recite a long poem about a farmer who was married to a true and loyal wife who helped him care for his cattle. The poem tells how one day in a storm she left a gate to the field open and the cattle escaped: The angry farmer threw terribly unkind words at his wife. When he was engaged in another task, she went out into the cold and snow to find the cows. When she didn't come home, he went out and found her frozen body. I used to cry whenever grandfather recited this poem, and I can only quote the last two lines from memory: "Boys flying kites haul in their white winged birds; but you can't do that when you're flying words." How often our too-late wail is "Why did I ever say that?" And how often do we need to say, "I have not loved you as I ought; will you forgive me?"

3. Love does not envy (13:4). There are two kinds of envy. One covets the possessions or position or talents of another person. This is difficult to avoid because it is a human thing. The second resents the fact that others should have what it doesn't; it does not so much want things for itself as wish that others did not have them.

We can see what a devastating thing envy is in the Body of Christ. It has been said, "Never tell a baker how good another baker is." Should we say, "Never tell a preacher how good another preacher is"? An envious person could even resent another's being used by God. Love, on the other hand, praises God for the gifts, talents and blessings that another has received. It recognizes God at work and is satisfied with what he has been given even though another seems more gifted.

4. Love does not boast (13:4). There is a beautiful word in Isaiah concerning the disposition of Christ. The prophet says, "He will not shout or cry out, or raise his voice in

the streets."[11] Commenting on this verse, Franz Delitzsch writes,

> Although (the servant of Jehovah) is certain of His
> divine call, and brings to the nations the highest and
> the best, His manner of appearing is nevertheless
> quiet, gentle, and humble; the very opposite of those
> lying teachers, who endeavored to exalt themselves
> by noisy demonstrations. . . . He requires no forced
> trumpeting.[12]

In other words, our Lord Jesus did not boast. The writer
of Proverbs reminds us, "Let another praise you, and not
your own mouth; someone else, and not your own lips."[13]

Love is not inflated with its own importance. It recognizes
that everything we are and have that is good comes to us
from our heavenly Father. Yet, while it does not boast, neither does it put on a false humility. A loving person is not
afraid to say a simple "Thank you," when he is praised for a
job well done.

5. Love is not proud (13:4),[14] or to put it positively, "Love
   is humble." Scripture tells us that "God opposes the
   proud but gives grace to the humble,"[15] that He dwells in
   the high and holy place and with him who is of a humble
   and contrite spirit.[16] Pride was Lucifer's downfall. Pride
   keeps sinners from being honest about their sins. Pride
   stands in the way of our saying, "I was wrong; will you
   forgive me?"

   I once went through a phase where I was trying to be
   humble. I would put myself down when praised; I would
   tell God over and over that I didn't want to be proud. I
   worked really hard at being humble. I was delivered
   from this terrible quest for humility when I came upon
   Alexander Whyte's definition of a humble man as one
   "who knows how proud he is." Humility is to know that
   the human heart is proud by nature, confesses that pride
   to the Lord and goes about its business without further

thought of trying to be humble. If he becomes conscious that he is being lifted up with pride, he confesses that sin and surrenders to Christ.

6. Love is not rude (13:5). Literally Paul says, "Love does not behave disgracefully, dishonorably or indecently." It seeks to manifest the gracious character and disposition so apparent in our Lord. My wife and I live in a condominium, and once a year we attend an owners' meeting. Everybody wants to speak his or her mind. Some speak with politeness and grace; others are rude and tactless. One woman tore into the condo board of directors (all volunteers) with outspoken, harsh and blunt speech. There was an element of truth in what she had to say, but oh my, how she said it! Love never forgets that courtesy, tact and politeness are lovely traits.

7. Love is not self-seeking (13:5). Selfishness is the opposite of *agape*. It demands its rights and its own way, unlike our loving Lord who, according to Paul, "did not consider equality with God something to be grasped, but made himself nothing [literally, emptied himself], taking the very nature of a servant. . . ." This, says Paul, is to be the Christian's mindset in his or her relationships with others.[17]

8. Love is not easily angered (13:5). Paul is speaking about selfish anger—the kind by which angry men or women seek to control others or to get their own way. Some things in this world ought to anger us. Our Lord was angry at the hypocrisy of those who resented His healing on the Sabbath.[18] We may very well be righteously indignant at injustice, the abuse of children or the plunder of the poor. But love, as Phillips translates it, "is not touchy."

9. Love keeps no record of wrongs (13:5). It refuses to hold grudges or bitterness or resentment but makes willful decisions to forgive. Love remembers the words of Scripture, "Be kind and compassionate to one another,

forgiving each other, just as in Christ God forgave you."[19]

Some years ago I was asked to visit a gentleman who was a patient in a local psychiatric hospital. After a few moments of general conversation, I asked him what he did for a living. His reply: "I was a farmer until my brother stole my farm!" Then he volunteered, "I will never forgive my brother." Evidently he would rather have suffered the "torture chamber"[20] of depression than settle the matter with his brother.

10. Love does not delight in evil (13:6). It finds no pleasure in unrighteousness but seeks to please God through obedience to His will. Neither does love gloat over others' sins and failures. It is a peculiar trait of human nature that we would rather hear of the misfortune of others than of their good fortune. Paul is saying that this is not a loving attitude.

11. Love rejoices with the truth (13:6). This could have several equally helpful applications. A person who loves God and people will rejoice when the truth of the gospel is proclaimed and gains ground in the world. A person who loves will rejoice when someone whose character has been maligned is vindicated and the truth is brought to light. Love will rejoice when someone who has been covering his or her sin confesses the truth in order to regain fellowship with God and fellow believers. Love rejoices in the truth wherever and however it is found!

12. Love always protects (13:7). A better translation would be "love covers all things."[21] In other words, love does not spread rumors or participate in idle gossip.

13. Love always trusts (13:7). When we love people, we want to trust them, to believe they are telling the truth. We expect good things from them even though circumstantial evidence would argue against it.

14. Love always hopes (13:7). It refuses to take failure as final; it is "the confidence which looks to ultimate triumph by the grace of God."[22]

15. Love always perseveres (13:7). Love endures life's trials and difficulties and turns them into blessings. George Matheson, the hymn writer who lost his sight and his fiancée, prayed that he might accept God's will, "not with dumb resignation, but with holy joy; not only with the absence of murmur, but with a song of praise."[23] Love perseveres not somehow, but triumphantly!

It is clear that only as the Holy Spirit works Christ's love in us can we begin to manifest the beautiful fruit called *agape*. God will never command us to love without providing the ability to obey the command.

The Permanence of Love (13:8-13)

Paul begins these final verses with the simple statement, "Love never fails." God is love, and as long as God exists, love, unlike certain temporary supernatural manifestations, will exist.

Prophecies (13:8) will be needful only as long as we do not perfectly know the will of God or need the encouragement or admonition that our human condition requires. Tongues will be helpful only as long as we are hindered in our praise or prayer by the limitations of our finite minds. The word of knowledge will be helpful only until that time when we shall "know fully, even as [we are] fully known" (13:12). These manifestations of the Spirit will pass away in that Day when "perfection comes" (13:10)—that glad moment when Christ, who is our life, appears and we appear with Him in glory.[24]

Paul uses two simple metaphors to illustrate his point. The first (13:11) is the picture of a child's speech and mentality compared with an adult's. A child's vocabulary and knowledge are limited. A child thinks narrowly, unable to grasp the full implications of a situation. He does not put the present moment in the context of all of life. But when he or she grows up, he or she has a larger vocabulary and can think and reason logically and in a whole-life context.

Paul is saying that we are spiritually in the age of childhood when we need the kind of help that adults do not need. There is coming an hour when we will fully know all we need to know without the assistance that the gifts of the Spirit bring. But one thing that both children and adults continue to need and give is love.

The second metaphor (13:12) refers to ancient mirrors, which reflected an often faint and fuzzy image. Paul is saying that in this present age, our perceptions of God and spiritual realities are faint, unclear and even distorted. We need the help that the gifts of the Spirit bring us. But a day is coming when we will see spiritual reality clearly, no longer through the veil of human flesh but in a face-to-face encounter with our Lord. Even in that day love will abide.

Whatever may disappear in the Day of Christ's appearing, it will not be love. Faith will be turned into sight, hope into the completed redemption of our bodies. What we only trusted for will become a visible reality, and what we only hoped for will become perfectly seen. But the love of God, shed in our hearts by the Holy Spirit, will go on forever. Love will never fail. Therefore, how important is John's exhortation to us:

> Dear friends, let us love one another, for love comes from God. Everyone who loves has been born of God and knows God. Whoever does not love does not know God, because God is love.[25]

Conclusion

What a heart-searching, powerful passage. What a careful examination of my motivation for service it calls for. Am I exercising the gift God has given me out of love, in order to glorify Him and help and bless others, or is there a secret desire to aggrandize myself, to receive the praise of men, to cover up some deep personal problem or to appear more spiritual than others? It is important to allow the Holy Spirit to purify our motives.

The Holy Spirit's work is to produce this lovely fruit of love in our lives. But if we would love with genuine *agape*, we must desire to love, and choose to allow the Spirit to effect this disposition of Christ in our renewed nature. In all of the eventualities of life, we must ask, "What would love do? How would love respond to this or that situation? What expression of love would be best for this person? What need does my brother really have which I can meet?" Love is a choice!

Endnotes

1. Barrett, 297.
2. John 15:12
3. p. 118.
4. Matthew 6:2-4
5. 2 Timothy 4:2
6. 2 Corinthians 6:6
7. Romans 2:4; see also 2 Peter 3:9
8. Ephesians 5:1
9. Cited in Barclay, 119.
10. 1 Thessalonians 5:14-15
11. Isaiah 42:2
12. *Commentary of the Old Testament*, vol. VII, "Isaiah" (Grand Rapids, MI: William B. Eerdmans Publishing Company, reprinted 1975), 175.
13. Proverbs 27:2
14. Here is that word that Paul has used so often in this letter—"puffed up."
15. 1 Peter 5:5

16. Isaiah 57:15

17. Philippians 2:6-7

18. Mark 3:5

19. Ephesians 4:32

20. In Matthew 18, Jesus tells the parable of an unforgiving servant who, because he refused to forgive a small debt owed by a fellow servant, incurred the wrath of his master and was delivered to the "torturers" (RSV).

21. See Kittel, vol. VII, 387. Cf. 1 Peter 4:8

22. Morris, 186.

23. Quoted in Barclay, 124.

24. Colossians 3:4. The view that the word "perfection" in verse 10 refers to the completion of the New Testament canon and that therefore certain gifts are only temporary in nature is clearly without any exegetical warrant. The context indicates that perfection refers to the day when we shall see face to face. It is the Day when our Lord Jesus returns in glory.

25. 1 John 4:7-8

CHAPTER 18

Edifying Worshipers

1 Corinthians 14:1-25

Follow the way of love and eagerly desire spiritual gifts, especially the gift of prophecy. For anyone who speaks in a tongue does not speak to men but to God. Indeed, no one understands him; he utters mysteries with his spirit. But everyone who prophesies speaks to men for their strengthening, encouragement and comfort. He who speaks in a tongue edifies himself, but he who prophesies edifies the church. I would like every one of you to speak in tongues, but I would rather have you prophesy. He who prophesies is greater than one who speaks in tongues, unless he interprets, so that the church may be edified.

Now, brothers, if I come to you and speak in tongues, what good will I be to you, unless I bring you some revelation or knowledge or prophecy or word of instruction? Even in the case of lifeless things that make sounds, such as the flute or harp, how will anyone know what tune is being played unless there is a distinction in the notes? Again, if the trumpet does not sound a clear call, who will get ready for battle? So it is with you. Unless you speak intelligible words with your tongue, how will anyone know what you are saying? You will just be speaking into the air. Undoubtedly there are all sorts of languages in the world, yet none of them is without meaning. If then I do not grasp the meaning of what someone is saying, I am a foreigner to the speaker, and he is a foreigner to me. So it is with you. Since you are eager to have spiritual gifts, try to excel in gifts that build up the church.

For this reason anyone who speaks in a tongue should pray that he may interpret what he says. For if I pray in a tongue, my spirit prays, but my mind is unfruitful. So what shall I do? I will pray with my spirit, but I will also pray with my mind; I will sing with my spirit, but I will also sing with my mind. If you are praising God with your spirit, how can one who finds himself among those who do not understand say "Amen" to your thanksgiving, since he does not know what you are saying? You may be giving thanks well enough, but the other man is not edified.

I thank God that I speak in tongues more than all of you. But in the church I would rather speak five intelligible words to instruct others than ten thousand words in a tongue.

Brothers, stop thinking like children. In regard to evil be infants, but in your thinking be adults. In the Law it is written:

"Through men of strange tongues
   and through the lips of foreigners
I will speak to this people,
   but even then they will not listen to me,"
says the Lord.

Tongues, then, are a sign, not for believers but for unbelievers; prophecy, however, is for believers, not for unbelievers. So if the whole church comes together and everyone speaks in tongues, and some who do not understand or some unbelievers come in, will they not say that you are out of your mind? But if an unbeliever or someone who does not understand comes in while everybody is prophesying, he will be convinced by all that he is a sinner and will be *judged by all, and the secrets of his heart will be laid bare. So he will fall down and worship God, exclaiming, "God is really among you!"*

Paul takes up his teaching concerning the gifts of the Spirit that he began in chapter 12. Evidently the somewhat chaotic situation in the Corinthian assembly made it necessary for him to deal more fully with two of those gifts, speaking in tongues (called *glossolalia*)[1] and prophecy. It seems that some of the Corinthian believers were unlovingly misusing the first gift with the result that others wanted to ban its use (14:39).

Times do not appear to have changed too much. Some in today's Church treat the gift of speaking in tongues as the chiefest of the gifts, *the* necessary mark of baptism in the Spirit, a sign of spiritual maturity. At the other extreme, some make the unprovable assumption that God withdrew the gift from the Church with the completion of the New Testament canon and that if it appears today, it is either demonic or fleshly. As a result it has become the source of much division. George Mallone humorously calls it "the biggest Christian friendship and oneness buster of the century."[2]

Both extremes in attitude are wrong. It would be better to believe that the gift of speaking in tongues is a good gift of the Holy Spirit, not the greatest, but a true gift not to be despised.

Words That Are Understood (14:1-13)

With those as basic assumptions, let us discover what Paul says that may help allay the fears of some and the biases of others. We see immediately (14:1) that the apostle insists the exercise of spiritual gifts in the assembly's worship services be surrounded with the genuine Christian love he described in chapter 13. In the same breath, he encourages believers to desire the gifts of the Spirit.[3]

Paul considers the gift of prophecy to be more important. A prophecy strengthens, encourages and comforts (14:3) and is given by the Holy Spirit through a member for edifying the assembly (14:5). It is not the same thing as regular preaching, although a sermon may contain prophetic words given immediately by the Spirit. It need not be prefaced by a "thus saith the Lord," but the hearers will know that they have heard the voice of God to them.

Paul admonishes the Thessalonians not to "treat prophecies with contempt," but to "test everything" and "hold on to the good."[4] Everything that purports to be prophecy must be tested against Scripture. If there is disagreement between the two, the spoken prophecy must be rejected. The purpose of the gift of prophecy is not to add to the written Word but to bring a helpful, contemporary message from our gracious Lord Jesus to a specific person, group or situation.

Several years ago our church decided to expand its facilities and engaged a fund-raising company and an architect/builder. When the new building design had been developed and the method of paying for it had been determined, a special meeting was called to present everything for congregational approval.

After the treasurer had finished describing how we would pay for the project, a woman stood, visibly agitated. She, with her husband, had recently come into our church from a charismatic congregation and professed to have the gift of prophecy. In an emotional voice, she said the elders had "gone down to Egypt" for their fund-raising plans and that we would be outside God's will were we to approve them. After she sat down the chairman thanked her and the meeting took up where it had left off.

The elders sensed that what purported to be a prophecy from God to our church was nothing more than one woman's opinion of our hiring a fundraiser. Her words were neither strengthening, encouraging or comforting and her manner was disrespectful. We discerned that her spirit was wrong, her prophecy false. We did not accept it as the will of God for our assembly.

The charisma of speaking in tongues may appropriately take place in the public assembly only if it is accompanied by an interpretation which all can understand. When that happens, the message given in tongues is equal in edifying value to a prophetic word (14:5).

I recall an instance in the loving circle of a church prayer meeting during a period in which the Holy Spirit had been reviving our fellowship. One member expressed a sense that the Holy Spirit had a word for us and asked permission to exercise the gift of tongues and interpretation. The members nodded approval, and the message was delivered and interpreted in a quiet and unemotional way. Though edifying, it seemed rather innocuous. We discovered later that a woman in the meeting received confirmation from the Lord through that prophetic gift of the Spirit concerning an important decision with which she was struggling.[5] How gracious and loving is our Lord to His children!

Incidentally one of the church elders came to me afterward with a Bible opened to First Corinthians 14, in the margin of which he had penned the words, "Not for today." He asked, "Is what happened here tonight what Paul is talking about in this chapter?" I replied that I thought it was. Pointing to his marginal notation he announced, "I think I'm going to have to scratch this!"

Paul emphasizes the importance of the assembly's understanding what is being said. To hear a message in tongues without the interpretation, he says, is like hearing music that has no meaningful variation in the sounds. No one will recognize the melody. This is especially true when the music, like the trumpet call to the army, is supposed to convey an important message to the troops. If the sound of the trumpet is unclear, the soldiers will not know what to do. So also a message given to the assembly in words that cannot be understood is quite useless. Therefore, says Paul, "anyone who speaks in a tongue should pray that he may interpret what he says" (14:6-13).

Words That Are Not Understood (14:14-18)

Throughout this passage, Paul describes the benefit of the

gift of tongues in private prayer. Arnold Bittlinger says about verses 2 and 14:

> Paul maintains that the Spirit dwelling in man speaks to God in a way that is incomprehensible to man. But because the Spirit dwells in us and infuses our whole being, our total person is caught up in this praying, which is more direct and total than prayer with the mind. Paul expresses this in Romans 8:26f as follows: "For we do not know how to pray as we ought, but the Spirit himself intercedes for us with sighs too deep for words. And He who searches the hearts of men knows what is the mind of the Spirit, because the Spirit intercedes for the saints according to the will of God."[6]

Praying in tongues, therefore, enables one to pray in the will of God, even though he may not know intellectually how he ought to pray in a given circumstance.

In verse 16, Paul speaks about "praising God with your spirit." At times our hearts are so full that we do not have sufficient words to worship and praise our God. It is then that the gift of "praying with the spirit"[7] enables us to "express the inexpressible."[8] Such praise in the Spirit may be either spoken or sung (14:15). One of my closest friends first began to exercise this gift in a beautiful song for which the Holy Spirit gave both the words and the melody. My friend was enveloped in a moving sense of the love of God as the song unfolded.

Again the gift of praying in tongues is said by Paul to be a spiritually self-edifying gift (14:4). Some have misinterpreted this verse to mean that Paul was discouraging the private use of tongues because he felt that edifying oneself was selfish. Jude, however, in his little letter exhorts believers to "build yourselves up in your most holy faith and pray in the Holy Spirit."[9] Surely if we are to edify others, we must ourselves be edified. There is nothing at all selfish about this.

Larry Christenson believes that by praying in tongues, a person is "built up in that part of his life where he most needs building up."[10]

For whatever reasons, Paul thanks God that he speaks in tongues more than all the Corinthians. We may rightly conclude that though this gift is only to be used in public assembly when accompanied by the companion gift of interpretation so that *all* will be built up; it may be used in private prayer as much and as often as one desires.[11]

Words That Are for a Sign (14:20-25)

One wise and colorful pastor friend charged some modern promoters of the more spectacular manifestations of the Spirit with "playing parlor games with the gifts of the Spirit." He felt they were using the gift of tongues like little children would use a new toy. Apparently the Corinthians were doing just that in their assembly. It appears from what Paul says that many were speaking in tongues at once, ignoring the more edifying gift of prophecy.

In 14:20 Paul admonishes them to stop being childish in their view of tongues. It is not to be regarded as an exciting and novel toy to be used indiscriminately. Quoting Isaiah 28:11-12, he implies a very serious connection between the gift of tongues and the judgment of God. The connection is not clear in the context, as the great variety of proposed interpretations indicate.[12]

But one thing is clear. Paul is warning the church that the gift of tongues is not something to play around with in their assemblies. Should unbelievers come into the church and hear everyone speaking in tongues at once, they would think the church was a madhouse (1 Corinthians 14:23) and damage would be done to the reputation of Christ. But if an unbeliever heard intelligible words of prophecy, he might more readily be convicted of his sin, recognize that he must stand before God the judge, be compelled to honestly face the truth about his own heart and fall on his knees before the awesome presence of God (14:24-25).

Conclusion

Believers who desire the deeper Christian life should not fear any genuinely Spirit-given manifestation. But everything that is spoken in the assembled church should be understood and edifying to the people. Therefore, unless it is interpreted (and is thus equivalent to prophecy), the gift of speaking or singing in tongues should be restricted to one's private prayer closet. There, alone with God, it becomes a vehicle for both praise and intercession.

Sometimes, as Paul says, "We do not know what we ought to pray." At this point words given by the Holy Spirit can assure one that he is praying in the will of God. Paul goes on to say, "And he who searches our hearts [i.e., God] knows the mind of the Spirit, because the Spirit intercedes for the saints in accordance with God's will."[13] While this gift is neither the necessary evidence of a person's being filled with the Spirit nor the greatest of the gifts of the Spirit, it is, nevertheless a valuable gift not to be feared, despised or relegated to the "apostolic age."

I close this chapter with the penetrating words of the late Dr. A.W. Tozer, former editor of *The Alliance Life* magazine:

> The Christian Church cannot rise to its true stature in accomplishing the purposes of God when its members operate largely through the gifts of nature, neglecting the true gifts and graces of the Spirit of God.
>
> Much of the religious activity we see in the churches is not the eternal working of the Eternal Spirit, but the mortal working of man's mortal mind—and that is raw tragedy!
>
> From what I see and sense in evangelical circles, I would have to say that about ninety percent of the religious work carried on in the churches is being done by ungifted members.
>
> I am speaking in this context of men and women

who know how to do many things but fail to display the spiritual gifts promised through the Holy Spirit.

This is one of the very evident ways in which we have slowed down the true working of God in His church and in the hearts of unbelieving men all around us—acknowledging and allowing ungifted members of the body to do religious work without possessing the genuine gifts of the Spirit. . . .

So brethren, the Spirit of God, His presence and His gifts are not only desirable in our Christian congregations, but absolutely imperative! . . .

The important thing is that the Holy Spirit desires to take men and women and control and use them as instruments and organs through which He can express Himself in the Body of Christ.[14]

Endnotes

1. See Bittlinger, p. 97, for an explanation of this word, that derives from the Greek phrase *en glossais lalein*, "to speak in languages."

2. George Mallone, *Those Controversial Gifts* (Downers Grove, IL: InterVarsity Press, 1983), 79.

3. The word translated "earnestly desire" is *zeloute* meaning, according to the lexicon, to "strive, desire, or exert oneself earnestly." The idea that there are some gifts of the Holy Spirit for which one may not humbly and sincerely ask seems to contradict Paul's word here.

4. 1 Thessalonians 5:20-21

5. It needs to be said that it is not usually wise to base important guidance decisions solely on such manifestations of the Spirit. These may be used to confirm the will of God that has already been discovered through the Scripture and the quiet voice of the Spirit in one's heart together with the wise advice of fellow believers.

6. p. 98. Arnold Bittlinger is a German scholar whose book was one of the first to be written outside Pentecostal literature by someone who has fairly wide experience of the manifestations of the Spirit in churches in Germany. *Gifts and Grace* is a fine commentary on First Corinthians 12-14.

7. Arthur Wallis, *Pray in the Spirit* (London and Eastbourne: Victory Press, 1970) offers the insight that not all prayer in the Spirit is prayer in tongues. Prayer in the Spirit is any prayer that the Spirit places within us. It may be in our own known language, in an unknown language or in no language at all, as the "groans" about which Paul speaks in Romans 8:26.

8. This expression is used by Paul Tournier in his book, *The Meaning of Persons*, to describe the need to carry the dialogue with God beyond the narrow limits of clearly intelligible language. It is cited by Larry Christenson, *Speaking in Tongues* (Minneapolis, MN: Dimension Books, 1968), 26. While there are certain aspects of Christenson's book that many of us would have difficulty accepting, yet on the whole it is a very sane and fair treatment of the subject.

9. Jude 20

10. p. 77. Without relegating the gifts of the Spirit to the realm of psychology, it is interesting to note that some psychiatrists believe that the gift of tongues also has psychologically edifying effects. Bittlinger, pp. 99-100, quotes a number of such doctors.

11. The idea that the manifestation of tongues on the Day of Pentecost was for evangelistic purposes is highly suspect. Peter preached his evangelistic sermon in Aramaic and was surely understood by all who heard since the response to the sermon was overwhelming.

12. For example, Calvin, p. 452, interprets the prophet Isaiah's words as meaning that Judah has been "visited

with such blindness and madness, that they no more understand God when was speaking to them, than they would some barbarian or foreigner, stammering in an unknown tongue—which is a dreadful curse." And by the use of this Old Testament quotation, Calvin thinks Paul is saying to the Corinthians, "Brethren, it is necessary to guard against that childishness, which is so severely reproved by the Prophet—that the word of God sounds in your ears without any fruit. Now, when you reject prophecy, which is placed within your reach, and prefer to stand amazed at empty sound, is not this voluntarily to incur the curse of God?"

Barclay, p. 131, interprets the passage as follows: "God, through his prophet, is threatening the people. Isaiah had preached to them in their own Hebrew language and they have not listened. Because of their disobedience, the Assyrians will come and conquer them and occupy their cities and then they will have to listen to language which they cannot understand. They will have to listen to their conquerors speaking unintelligible things; and not even that terrible experience will make an unbelieving people turn to God. So Paul uses the argument that tongues were meant for a hard-hearted and unbelieving people and were, in the end, ineffective to them."

Leon Morris, p. 197, suggests that Paul means "that, as those who had refused to heed the prophet were punished by hearing speech that was not intelligible to them, so would it be in his day. Those who would not believe would hear 'tongues,' and not be able to understand their wonderful meaning."

13. Romans 8:26-27

14. Taken from *Tragedy in the Church: The Missing Gifts*, chapter 3, p. 33.

CHAPTER 19

Ordering Worship

1 Corinthians 14:26-40

What then shall we say, brothers? When you come together, everyone has a hymn, or a word of instruction, a revelation, a tongue or an interpretation. All of these must be done for the strengthening of the church. If anyone speaks in a tongue, two—or at the most three—should speak, one at a time, and someone must interpret. If there is no interpreter, the speaker should keep quiet in the church and speak to himself and God.

Two or three prophets should speak, and the others should weigh carefully what is said. And if a revelation comes to someone who is sitting down, the first speaker should stop. For you can all prophesy in turn so that everyone may be instructed and encouraged. The spirits of prophets are subject to the control of prophets. For God is not a God of disorder but of peace.

As in all the congregations of the saints, women should remain silent in the churches. They are not allowed to speak, but must be in submission, as the Law says. If they want to inquire about something, they should ask their own husbands at home; for it is disgraceful for a woman to speak in the church.

Did the word of God originate with you? Or are you the only people it has reached? If anybody thinks he is a

prophet or spiritually gifted, let him acknowledge that
what I am writing to you is the Lord's command. If he ig-
nores this, he himself will be ignored.

Therefore, my brothers, be eager to prophesy, and do not
forbid speaking in tongues. But everything should be done
in a fitting and orderly way.

It was Sunday morning in Corinth, and the Parmenides family was getting ready for church. Little Billy excitedly remarked, "I wonder what will happen in church this morning!"

"Who knows," replied his nineteen-year-old sister, Elizabeth, "but if it was like last Sunday, there'll be chaos!"

"Hush, daughter," said Mrs. Parmenides. "That's no way to speak about the assembly of the saints."

"Well, you know it's true, Mother. I invited Phidius to come to church with us last Sunday. He doesn't believe as we do, and he got up and left and vows he'll never return. He says those people are out of their minds. There were people jabbering in foreign languages all over the place, and I couldn't understand a word they were saying. And the prophets were all talking at once. I didn't get a thing out of the service—all three hours of it."

Father Permenides spoke up, "Well, Elizabeth, be patient. I have written to our beloved Apostle Paul and asked his advice. I expect he'll reply shortly with an answer to our problems."

"Well," said Elizabeth, "I'll give it another Sunday, but if things don't change, I'm not going to church anymore."

"I beg your pardon," said her father, "you'll be going to church with us as long as you're living in this home!"

Paul's letter came, and it was long. And when they read sections 12-14 in the manuscript, there were a lot of red faces. But things were much more orderly in the assembly. They were blessed to have that letter.

Instruction to Speakers (14:26-33a)

Paul gives the church some simple, clear instruction concerning their use of the gifts of the Spirit in the assembly. Those first-century worship services were much less structured than ours today; perhaps they were more like an informal small-group meeting in someone's home. Each person would have opportunity to contribute in some fashion to the service. One might suggest a hymn;[1] another might give a word of Christian teaching; another a revelation;[2] still another might have a message in tongues; and someone else might interpret. Whatever the contribution, each was to remember that the purpose was to build up the Body of Christ (14:26), not self-glory.

Within such an atmosphere of spontaneous informality, Paul instructs the church to have some minimal structure. The occasions for tongues speaking was to be limited to two or three, and only if an interpretation was assured (14:27, 28). Two or three prophets could speak one at a time, giving place to each other in a spirit of courteous love, knowing that they were not forced against their wills to speak, but were quite able to stop when another was ready (14:29-32).[3]

What Paul envisaged for their worship services was neither rigid order nor disorganized confusion, but a dynamic orderliness resulting from each member's listening to the voice of the Spirit and each regarding the other person better than himself. The resulting condition would be peace.

I was once asked to address a weeknight service in a neighboring church on "The Gifts of the Spirit." A number of old-time Pentecostal folk were there, and when I suggested the need for leadership to keep orderliness in services where audible gifts of the Spirit are in operation, one dear lady spoke up in a rather sharp voice and demanded, "Young man, who is in charge in your services, you or the Holy Ghost?"

She had been raised in a church environment in which sermons, testimonies or whatever was happening at the moment could be interrupted by messages in tongues. To stop such manifestations was called "touching the ark."[4] My reply to the elderly lady's question was, "Both of us." Our text makes it clear that there is no contradiction between dynamic manifestations of the Spirit's gifts and peaceful orderliness aided by Spirit-led leadership.

Instruction to Women (14:33b-36)

Having instructed the tongues speakers and the prophets, Paul now has a word for the women of the Corinthian assembly—a word that he has given to all the congregations (14:33b). Recall that in 11:5 he instructs women who pray or prophesy in the assembly to do so with covered heads. How does one reconcile this obvious permission for women to pray or prophesy with the command that they should keep silent? Scholars present varying views,[5] but it appears likely that Paul did not want the Corinthian women to do anything that would fail to reflect their God-ordained submission to their husbands,[6] detract from the dynamic orderliness of the service through unnecessary conversation or otherwise bring the cause of Christ into disrepute.

His instruction in First Timothy 2:11-15 throws light on our text. There he forbids women to "teach or to have authority over [men]." While Paul has no hesitation in allowing women upon whom the Spirit of God rests to pray or prophesy in the assembly, he is not about to allow them to take the role of leadership or to teach publicly.

Instructions to the Spiritually Gifted (14:36-40)

Paul's somewhat ironic inquiry, "Did the word of God originate with you? Or are you the only people it has reached?" (14:36), would indicate that the practices he has been rebuking had been taking place in the church. After all we have seen about the pride of the Corinthians, this should not surprise us. But they must not be allowed to think they alone know what is acceptable Christian behavior.

Paul concludes his instruction on the manifestations of the Spirit by enforcing his spiritual authority, indicating that any true prophet in the Corinthian assembly would readily agree that what their apostle had commanded was indeed the word of the Lord.[7] No higher claim could be made. And anyone who would speak a different word was to be ignored[8] (14:37-38).

It would appear that some of the more conservative members of the assembly, disturbed at the over-stress placed on the gift of tongues, wanted to ban their use altogether. Paul vetoes this suggestion and encourages the church members to "be eager to prophecy, and do not forbid speaking in tongues. But everything should be done in a fitting and orderly way" (14:39-40).

Conclusion

We might apply the passage before us to our church life today by affirming that believers who desire the deeper life in Christ will be concerned that their practice of corporate worship correspond in a modern setting to the counsel given by Paul. For one thing, our worship services must be alive in the Spirit. This does not imply any kind of slipshod, unrehearsed, boisterous assembly, but rather a service in which there is such a consciousness of God's presence that hearts are lifted up to Him to true adoration and joyful praise.

Second, our text indicates something of the content of a God-honoring worship service. Our services should be uncomplicated and uncluttered with elements that detract from the knowledge of God. Worship, in both classic and appropriate contemporary hymnody, should focus on His triune Person and holy character. A lady once complained to her pastor that she did not like his choice of hymns for the service. He replied, "I did not choose them for you, but for God." The hymns (sung prayers to God) that are used in our worship services should be those that we can sing with honesty, no matter how we feel or what mood we may be in.

Our prayers to God (spoken or sung) must be balanced by the faithful hearing of His Word to us. Regular, expository teaching and preaching of the Scripture must be the diet that we feed upon each Sunday. It is not necessary, perhaps not even advisable, that the gifts of tongues and interpretation be manifest in a Sunday morning worship service. The heterogeneous complexion of the average congregation would make this inadvisable. But we should be able to leave the service knowing that we have heard the voice of God. There should be a prophetic note in our preaching.

Both male and female participants in our worship services should put themselves under the Lordship of the Spirit of Christ. The elders who lead the service should be "in the Spirit"; the men or women who participate in any public way should be people of good report and of a humble and unpretentious demeanor.

It is awesome to remember that each time we meet together in assembly, our Lord and Savior Jesus Christ is there with us.[9] A consciousness of His presence in our midst would influence both the content and delivery of the preacher's sermon and the congregation's comportment and response to truth.

Endnotes

1. The word used is *psalmos*. This might mean one of the Old Testament psalms or it could mean a song of praise or worship composed by the singer. Writing to the Ephesians, Paul instructs them to use "psalms and hymns (*humoi*) and spiritual songs (*ode pneumatike*)" in their worship and praise. A hymn is a sung prayer addressed to the Trinity; a spiritual song is likely a song sung spontaneously as the Spirit gave words and melody.

2. This might be in the form of a word of prophecy or sometimes recounting a vision, with its meaning.

3. In connection with the manifestations of the Spirit that involve spoken words, as in tongues or prophecy or interpretation of tongues, it is important to recognize that

unlike the influence of demonic spirits, the Holy Spirit does not "possess" the speaker to force him to speak against his will or without his control. No one *has* to speak in tongues; no one *has* to prophesy. The speaker can stop at any time. No prophet in Corinth had to continue speaking because the Spirit compelled him to do so.

4. The expression is taken from Second Samuel 6:6, where Uzza "reached out and took hold of the ark of God, because the oxen stumbled." This was evidently human interference in a God-ordained procedure.

5. Here are a few: Morris, p. 201, thinks that Paul is forbidding women to be instructors in the church and thus discredit Christianity in the eyes of most people. Moffat, quoted by Morris, p. 201, takes the view that this is a prohibition of "matrons taking part in the discussion or interpretation of what had been said by some prophet or teacher during the service." Barrett, p. 232, suggests the possibility that "in the interests of peace and good order he could command the women to be silent, precisely as he could give orders for a male prophet to be silent if his continued speech was likely to prove unedifying." Keener, pp. 70, 88, thinks Paul is addressing relatively uneducated women who were disrupting the service with irrelevant questions. He contextualizes this to say for us that those who do not know the Bible very well should not set the pace for learning in the Christian congregation, but should get private instruction! Calvin, quoted by Morris, p. 202, thinks that Paul is forbidding women to speak in a regular church service.

6. Does he have Genesis 3:16 in mind when he says women are to be in submission as *the Law says*? If not, then it is almost impossible to know to what other Old Testament passage he may be referring.

7. The word "Lord" in verse 37 is in an emphatic position in the sentence.

8. Or some manuscript evidence would have the phrase read, "let him be ignorant," or "he will be disregarded"—a reference evidently to the day of judgment.

9. According to his promise of Matthew 18:20.

CHAPTER 20

Witnessing the Saving Gospel

1 Corinthians 15:1-11

Now, brothers, I want to remind you of the gospel I preached to you, which you received and on which you have taken your stand. By this gospel you are saved, if you hold firmly to the word I preached to you. Otherwise, you have believed in vain.

For what I received I passed on to you as of first importance: that Christ died for our sins according to the Scriptures, that he was buried, that he was raised on the third day according to the Scriptures, and that he appeared to Peter, and then to the Twelve. After that, he appeared to more than five hundred of the brothers at the same time, most of whom are still living, though some have fallen asleep. Then he appeared to James, then to all the apostles, and last of all he appeared to me also, as to one abnormally born.

For I am the least of the apostles and do not even deserve to be called an apostle, because I persecuted the church of God. But by the grace of God I am what I am, and his grace to me was not without effect. No, I worked harder than all of them—yet not I, but the grace of God that was with me. Whether, then, it was I or they, this is what we preach, and this is what you believed.

Some years ago I was seated in my church study when a soldier whom I had never seen before appeared in the doorway. He announced, "I am thinking of becoming a Christian; what should I do?" I took a copy of the New Testament from my bookshelf, handed him the book and replied, "Take this home, and when you have finished reading the four Gospels, come back and we'll talk." He thanked me and left.

I did not know whether he would return, but several weeks later he reappeared, sat down in front of me and without any preliminary niceties declared, "You are asking me to believe that a man died and rose again. I don't think I can do that." He had caught hold of the essential truth of the gospel! I encouraged him to go home and read the documents once more before making up his mind and was surprised when he returned. This time he stated, "It appears that there is some kind of commitment I have to make."

How powerful is the unadorned Word of God! How mighty is the good news of the historically verified death, burial and resurrection of the man, Christ Jesus!

During his visit to Athens, the Apostle Paul was escorted to the Court of the Areopagus to give an account of his unusual philosophy. He concluded his sermon with these words:

> Therefore, since we are God's offspring, we should not think that the divine being is like gold or silver or stone—an image made by man's design and skill. In the past God overlooked such ignorance, but now he commands all people everywhere to repent. For he has set a day when he will judge the world with justice by the man he has appointed. *He has given proof of this to all men by raising him from the dead* [italics mine].
>
> Luke tells us that "When they heard about the resurrection of the dead, some of them sneered, but others said, 'We want to hear you again on this subject.' "[1]

The resurrection of the dead was a concept foreign to the philosophy of Greece. Immortality of the soul, yes. The philosopher Plato, whose writings have greatly influenced Christian theology, advanced a series of arguments for the soul's immortality. But the biblical concept of bodily resurrection was something else altogether.[2]

It becomes clear as one reads First Corinthians 15 that some in the church were more Platonic than biblical in their view of man's immortality. This, for Paul, is a heresy he answers with his magnificent treatise on the Christian doctrine of the resurrection of the body.

The Gospel Message Received (15:1-2)

Paul's intention in the first eleven verses is to draw the Corinthians' attention[3] to the fact that the resurrection of Jesus Christ was an indispensable part of the gospel message. This gospel, he told the Galatians, "[was] not something that man made up." Nor was it something he received "from any man, nor was (he) taught it; rather, (he) received it by revelation from Jesus Christ."[4] He feels so strongly about this that he can pronounce a curse on anyone who would pervert this gospel.[5]

The gospel he had received from the Lord Jesus he had faithfully proclaimed to the Corinthians; they in turn had received it from him.[6] On it they had "taken [their] stand"[7] and, holding firmly to its truth, they "[were] being saved."[8]

The Gospel Message Transmitted (15:3-7)

The saving message Paul proclaimed consisted of four distinct historical facts that, taken together, constituted the content of apostolic preaching.

1. "Christ died for our sins according to the Scriptures" (15:3). His was a real death. In the Garden of Gethsemane He had struggled with the prospect of dying the cruel death He knew lay before him.[9] But He had surrendered to His Father's will and endured the shameful death of the cross "for our sins." As Paul tells the

Corinthians in another letter, "God made him who had no sin to be sin [or a sin offering] for us, so that in him we might become the righteousness of God."[10] Here is a straight exchange—our sin imputed to the sinless Christ; His perfect righteousness imputed to us sinners. The apostle Peter tells us, "[Christ] himself bore our sins in his body on the tree, so that we might die to sins and live for righteousness."[11]

To demonstrate that the death of Christ was in God's eternal plan, Paul adds the words "according to the Scriptures." Perhaps he has in mind that great "suffering servant" passage, Isaiah 53, that tells us, "We all, like sheep, have gone astray, each of us has turned to his own way; and the LORD has laid on him the iniquity of us all";[12] or that vivid messianic Psalm 22, in which the psalmist cries out the words our Lord spoke on the cross, "My God, my God, why have you forsaken me?"[13]

2. ". . . that he was buried" (15:4). If it seems unnecessary to specifically mention his burial, we must remember that for the Hebrews, burial was proof of death. Joseph, a rich man from Arimathea who also was a disciple of Jesus, had asked Pilate if he might bury the body of his Master. Upon receiving the governor's permission, he placed the body in a new tomb cut out of the rock and sealed the tomb with a large stone.[14] Pilate ordered his seal placed on the stone and a guard be posted to preclude anyone from stealing the body.[15] How beautifully Paul's mention of Christ's burial adds a greater significance to the fact of the empty tomb.[16]

3. ". . . that he was raised[17] on the third day according to the Scriptures" (15:4). Early in the morning, loving women went to look at the tomb. To their amazement, an angelic visitor announced, "He is not here; he has risen, just as he said."[18] They were instructed to pass the wonderful news along to the disciples.

The resurrection of Jesus was as essential for the salvation of men as His death. Paul tells the Romans that "[Christ] was delivered over to death for our sins and *was raised to life for our justification*" (emphasis added).[19] Implicit in this statement is the truth that His resurrection demonstrated that He had lived without sin and did not, therefore, deserve death; that His sinlessness qualified Him as a worthy substitute for us; and that God was perfectly satisfied with His death as an atonement for sin.

4. " . . . and that he appeared. . . ." (15:5-8). The Gospel writers make much of our Lord's post-resurrection appearances to His disciples. Luke records that "[a]fter his suffering, he showed himself to these men and gave many convincing proofs that he was alive. He appeared to them over a period of forty days and spoke about the kingdom of God."[20] Paul mentions six such appearances; the first five are (1) "to Peter" (perhaps to give him assurance that his sin of denial had been forgiven); (2) to "the Twelve" (a technical name for the remaining apostles); (3) to "more than five hundred of the brothers at the same time, most of whom are still living" (and could all testify to the fact that Jesus was alive); (4) "to James" (probably the Lord's brother); (5) to "all the apostles" (likely at the time of His ascension).[21]

The Gospel Riches Observed (15:8-11)

The sixth appearance mentioned is to Paul, "as to one abnormally born."[22] Intent on persecuting the Christians, Paul is on his way to Damascus with authorization to arrest them when he is stricken to the ground by a light flashing around him. He hears a voice saying, "Saul, Saul, why do you persecute me?" Upon inquiring as to the identity of the voice, he discovers that he has come face to face with the Lord Jesus, whom he had scorned and rejected.

Paul considers himself to be "the least of the apostles," not deserving of being designated an apostle because of his persecution of the Church (15:9). But the exalted Lord in His great grace had condescended to choose him, unworthy as he felt himself to be, to the high calling of "apostle of Christ Jesus" (1:1). By God's grace at work in him, Paul had labored at his calling harder than all the other apostles (15:10). He never tired of giving his testimony whenever and wherever opportunity presented itself.

Conclusion

Christ's empty tomb and subsequent appearances present unassailable proof of His bodily resurrection. This event is at the heart of the Christian gospel. Christians believe the resurrection of Christ is more than a holy history "myth" that has lovely implications, as some theologians would have us believe. They tell us the story is symbolic of the ideas that truth is stronger than error, good stronger than evil, love stronger than hate. The Christian faith is built, they tell us, around this inspiring symbol of resurrection.

Paul could never have tolerated such thought. The bodily resurrection of Jesus of Nazareth is a witnessed fact of history. The documentary evidence for it is as well, or better, attested as any other historical event.

It is not without great cause and joy that believers on the Lord Jesus observe Easter, the greatest of all the celebrations of the Christian calendar. Good Friday, that day when everything seemed to go wrong, gives place to a glorious resurrection morning. We firmly believe the words that the Apostle Peter proclaimed to the gathered men of Israel.

> This man was handed over to you by God's set purpose and foreknowledge; and you, with the help of wicked men, put him to death by nailing him to the cross. But God raised him from the dead, freeing him from the agony of death, because it was impossible for death to keep its hold on him.[23]

And we sing with all our hearts,

"Christ the Lord is risen today," Alleluia!
Sons of men and angels say. Alleluia!
Raise your joys and triumphs high; Alleluia!
Sing, ye heavens, and earth reply: Alleluia!

Love's redeeming work is done, Alleluia!
Fought the fight, the battle won; Alleluia!
Death in vain forbids Him rise, Alleluia!
Christ has opened Paradise. Alleluia!

Soar we now where Christ has led, Alleluia!
Following our exalted Head; Alleluia!
Made like Him, like Him we rise; Alleluia!
Ours the cross, the grave, the skies. Alleluia![24]

Endnotes

1. Acts 17:29-32

2. For an excellent summary of the biblical doctrine of immortality, see James Orr, *The Christian View of God and the World* (Grand Rapids, MI: William B. Eerdmans Publishing Company, 1954), 198-199.

3. The verb is *gnorizo*, essentially meaning "to cause to know."

4. Galatians 1:11-12

5. Galatians 1:8

6. *Paralabete* is in the aorist tense, pointing to a single act in the past. They likely believed the message of the gospel at the point it was first preached to them. *Paralabete* was the verb specifically employed to denote the receiving of something which was delivered by tradition. See F.F. Bruce, *Commentary on the Epistle to the Colossians* (Grand Rapids, MI: William B. Eerdmans Publishing Company, 1975), 226.

7. The tense of the verb, *hestekate*, is the Greek perfect. This points to an action in the past that has ongoing re-

sults. They took their stand, and they are still taking a stand on the gospel. It appears from the chapter that some of them were in danger of reneging on their stand, but Paul always thinks the best of his converts.

8. The Greek present tense indicates continuous action. The Scripture uses the word "saved" in three tenses— past (salvation is once for all); present (it is progressive as in 1:18); future (our salvation will be complete when Christ comes in glory [Romans 5:9]).

9. The Christian who rests assured of his salvation does not fear death; but he may very well fear the process of dying. So it was with our Lord Jesus.

10. 2 Corinthians 5:21

11. 1 Peter 2:24

12. Isaiah 53:6

13. Barrett, p. 239, points out, "It may well be that the general allusion to the Scriptures was made before specific passages were alleged in support of it. Christian conviction saw in the death of Christ a divine act that must have been foretold because it was a manifestation of the eternal will of God; out of this conviction arose the search of the Old Testament which in due course produced an armory of testimonies."

14. Matthew 27:57f

15. Matthew 27:65–66

16. See Morris, 205.

17. There is a lovely nuance here in the original tense of the verb "was raised." In contrast to "died" (aorist tense) and "was buried" (also aorist), "was raised" is in the perfect tense, which in Greek implies that the raising happened and remains in force. Christ died, but He is not dead; He was buried, but He is not now in the grave; He was raised, and He is alive today.

18. Matthew 28:6

19. Romans 4:25

20. Acts 1:3

21. Acts 1:1ff

22. The words are *to ektromati*, literally "an untimely birth" or "a miscarriage." Arndt and Gingrich, in their lexicon, p. 246, say that the word was used as a term of abuse, and that perhaps Paul is "taking up an insult . . . hurled at him by his opponents."

23. Acts 2:23-24

24. Charles Wesley, 1707-1788.

CHAPTER 21

Defending the Resurrection Doctrine

1 Corinthians 15:12-34

But if it is preached that Christ has been raised from the dead, how can some of you say that there is no resurrection of the dead? If there is no resurrection of the dead, then not even Christ has been raised. And if Christ has not been raised, our preaching is useless and so is your faith. More than that, we are then found to be false witnesses about God, for we have testified about God that he raised Christ from the dead. But he did not raise him if in fact the dead are not raised. For if the dead are not raised, then Christ has not been raised either. And if Christ has not been raised, your faith is futile; you are still in your sins. Then those also who have fallen asleep in Christ are lost. If only for this life we have hope in Christ, we are to be pitied more than all men.

But Christ has been raised from the dead, the firstfruits of those who have fallen asleep. For since death came through a man, the resurrection of the dead comes also through a man. For as in Adam all die, so in Christ all will be made alive. But each in his own turn: Christ, the firstfruits; then, when he comes, those who belong to him. Then the end will come, when he hands over the kingdom to God the Father after he has destroyed all dominion, authority and power. For he must reign until he has put

all his enemies under his feet. The last enemy to be de-
stroyed is death. For he "has put everything under his
feet." Now when it says that "everything" has been put
under him, it is clear that this does not include God him-
self, who put everything under Christ. When he has done
this, then the Son himself will be made subject to him who
put everything under him, so that God may be all in all.

Now if there is no resurrection, what will those do who
are baptized for the dead? If the dead are not raised at all,
why are people baptized for them? And as for us, why do
we endanger ourselves every hour? I die every day—I
mean that, brothers—just a surely as I glory over you in
Christ Jesus our Lord. If I fought wild beasts in Ephesus
for merely human reasons, what have I gained? If the dead
are not raised,

> *"Let us eat and drink,*
>   *for tomorrow we die."*

Do not be misled: "Bad company corrupts good charac-
ter." Come back to your senses as you ought, and stop sin-
ning; for there are some who are ignorant of God—I say
this to your shame.

I was riding between two prairie cities with a pastor who told me his doubts about the virgin birth, the literal resurrection and the divinity of Jesus of Nazareth. "What possible difference would it make to the gospel if none of these dogmas [his word] were literally true?" he demanded to know. "Are not these stories devised by Jesus' followers to enhance His reputation and make Him out to be a very special servant of God?"

Wondering what "good news" he had to proclaim to his congregation, I asked, "What is your 'gospel' message?" He replied that he believed God loves everyone, and that in the end everyone would be in heaven. I discovered (I confess, not to my surprise) that he had no concept of sin, atonement or propitiation, no understanding of resurrection and no comprehension of God's wrath. He had stripped the gospel of its essential truth and was preaching impotent sermons on morality and social change that assumed the inherent goodness rather than the depravity of mankind. His ideas had no need for a virgin-born, divine, crucified and resurrected Christ.

The Logical Confirmation (15:12-19; 29-34)

But the doctrines my friend denied were the heart of Paul's gospel. Now Paul presents his reasoning for believing in the bodily resurrection of the dead. How could anyone in the Corinthian assembly who believed that Christ had been raised from the dead[1] say there was no such thing as a resurrection of the dead? If it happened once, only a mistaken logic would conclude that it could not happen again (15:12).

If there is no such thing as a resurrection, then it would have been impossible for Christ to have been raised (15:13). Paul is calling for logical consistency. If one is true, the other must be true; if one is false, the other must be false.

Let us assume there is no resurrection from the dead and that Christ did not rise. What are the implications of such an unthinkable thought?

Paul sees eight. If Christ did not rise from the dead, then it follows that:

1. "Our preaching is useless . . ." (15:14). That is to say, what we preach has no redeeming content.[2] Take the resurrection out of the gospel and it is no longer "the power of God for the salvation of everyone who believes. . . ."[3]

2. ". . . and so is your faith" (literally "empty also your faith"). "The faith of the Corinthians depended on the gospel which had elicited it. If that gospel was a sham, then so was the faith it produced."[4]

3. ". . . we are then found to be false witnesses about God" (15:15). If Christ was not raised from the dead, all the apostles were caught in a lie about God, a very serious

matter. They had given false testimony, crediting God with a deed He did not do.

4. ". . . your faith is futile; you are still in your sins" (15:17). If God had not raised Jesus, it would have meant that Christ was condemned to suffer the "wages of sin,"[5] and had not really qualified as a spotless sacrifice to make atonement for sin. Thus the Corinthians could not have been justified through faith; their faith would have been fruitless—unable to secure a just pardon.

5. "Then those also who have fallen asleep in Christ are lost" (15:18). If Christ were still dead, death would be something other than "falling asleep" in Him. Both He and those who had believed in His resurrection would have perished. The Christian hope of immortality rests squarely upon the fact of Christ's resurrection. If this were discovered to be a lie, all hope of eternal life would be gone.

6. " . . . we are to be pitied more than all men" (15:19). Believers in Jesus were probably the most ill-treated people of Paul's day. They had set their hopes on the Day when they would be fully compensated for the sufferings they had endured for Christ's sake. If this world were all there was, anybody would be better off than Christians.

7. ". . . why are people baptized for [the dead]?" (15:29). Evangelical scholars usually think that Paul is using an *ad hominen* argument. That is to say, if the Corinthians believe in this practice, they are destroying their own case against the resurrection.[6]

8. ". . . why do we endanger ourselves every hour?" (15:30). What is the point of our facing tribulation and death for the sake of a lie?

With unrelenting logic, Paul has presented the dreadful implications of the non-resurrection of Jesus Christ. All hope of eternal life is demolished. Sin and death reign forever. Alas, there is no ultimate meaning to life or death.

The Seed-Plant Illustration (15:20-23)

Paul presents a resounding affirmation of the resurrection of Christ, of which he has no doubt. He had talked with eye-witnesses; he had come face to face with the glorified Christ, who, on the road to Damascus, had interrupted his designs to persecute Christians (15:8). This encounter qualified him to be an apostle.

But the resurrection of Christ also assures the resurrection of all in Him. Paul elaborates this first by the motif of the firstfruits (15:20), which comes from the Mosaic Law.

Israeli farmers were instructed to "[c]elebrate the Feast of Harvest with the firstfruits of the crops you sow in your field" and to "[b]ring the best of the firstfruits of your soil to the house of the LORD your God."[7] Again they were commanded, "When you enter the land I am going to give you and you reap its harvest, bring to the priest a sheaf of the first grain you harvest" and "[f]rom wherever you live, bring two loaves made of two-tenths of an ephah of fine flour, baked with yeast, as a wave offering of firstfruits to the LORD."[8]

The "firstfruits" was the first installment of the crop, and foreshadowed and pledged the ultimate offering of the whole. The resurrection of Christ, the first to rise from the dead, never to die again, is the pledge and proof of the resurrection of His people.

The "Representative" Conception (15:21-22)

Second, Paul develops the concept of the many in the one to show that the resurrection of Christ implies the resurrection of all believers. This concept, perhaps difficult for Western man to comprehend, is deeply embedded in Oriental thought.[9] Put simply it means that the entire human race is represented in two men—Adam and Christ.

I once taught a series of morning Bible studies at a Chinese youth conference, teaching from the letter to the Romans. One morning, I was unfolding the depths of 5:12-19—"Death through Adam, Life through Christ." I was

concerned that my audience might not comprehend the concept of the one in the many, which is central to Paul's argument in that passage. I need not have feared. A young
Chinese student came to me and assured me that the Chinese had this concept in their thought.

In our text it amounts to this: that the whole human race
(the many) is embodied in Adam (the one), and all believers,
the new race (the many), are included in Christ (the one).
Thus Adam's sin and the resulting death are imputed to all
men; and Christ's righteousness and eternal life are reckoned
to all believers (15:21-22).[10] Thus the resurrection of Christ
insures the resurrection of all who believe.[11]

The Temporal Sequence (15:23-28)

Paul goes on to say that the resurrection of Christ and the
resurrection of believers do not occur at the same time.
While Christ Jesus has already been raised from the dead,
believers patiently await their turn (15:23).[12] The resurrection of the "dead in Christ" and the clothing of living believers with immortality (15:53) will take place, Paul says, at
Christ's coming to establish His kingdom (15:23). This
"coming" (*parousia*) is vividly described in Paul's first letter
to the Thessalonians:

> For the Lord himself will come down from heaven,
> with a loud command, with the voice of the archangel
> and with the trumpet call of God, and the dead in
> Christ will rise first. After that, we who are still alive
> and are left will be caught up with them in the clouds
> to meet the Lord in the air. And so we will be with
> the Lord forever.[13]

Thereupon Christ Jesus our Lord, whose consequent
earthly reign will eventuate in the destruction of all God's
enemies— "all dominion, authority and power" that has ever
set itself up in opposition to God, including death itself
(15:25-26)—our Lord Christ will hand over His kingdom to

the Father (15:24), and the Son will become subject to Father "so that God may be all in all" (15:28). Hallelujah!

Conclusion

How every redeemed heart must long for that Day when "the kingdoms of this world become the kingdom of our God and of His Christ, and He shall reign forever and ever." I love the fifth stanza of Francis Havergal's hymn, "Thou Art Coming, O My Saviour."

> Oh, the joy to see Thee reigning—Thee, my own
>   beloved Lord!
> Every tongue Thy name confessing; Worship, honor,
>   glory, blessing Brought to Thee with one accord—
> Thee, my Master and my Friend, vindicated
>   and enthroned,
> Unto earth's remotest end, Glorified, adored and
>   owned![14]

"Vindicated!" When He was on earth, He was accused by unbelievers of being a deceiver. Throughout the following centuries, He has not been given His due. His deity, His Lordship, His right to reign have all been denied by the majority. But some day our Lord Jesus Christ will be vindicated. Who He really is will be made fully manifest to the universe. Our Lord is not only our Savior, Sanctifier and Healer, He is unquestionably our Coming King.

And we who have been united to Him and have known the fellowship of His sufferings will also "appear with him in glory"[15] and reign forever with Him! The Apostle John tells us:

> The reason the world does not know us is that it did not know him. Dear friends, now we are children of God, and what we will be has not yet been made known. But we know that when he appears, we shall be like him, for we shall see him as he is. Everyone

who has this hope in him purifies himself, just as he is pure.[16]

Brothers and sisters, His Day and ours is coming!

Endnotes

1. Evidently, according to 15:1-2, the Corinthian Christians were willing to concede that the resurrection of Jesus was part of the gospel to be believed.

2. The word translated "useless" is *kenos*, which means "vain" or "empty." In the original Greek it comes at the first of the clause for emphasis—"empty is our preaching."

3. Romans 1:16

4. Morris, 210.

5. Romans 6:23

6. Morris, p. 219, states that between thirty and forty explanations have been given for this verse! According to Barrett, p. 393, the most common view is that "Paul is referring to some kind of vicarious baptism, in which a Christian received baptism on behalf of someone, perhaps a friend or relative, who had died without being baptized. There is evidence for some such rite among various heretics."

   Chrysostum, cited by Barrett, p. 393, describes how "when a catechumen among (the Marcionites) dies, they hide a living man under the dead man's bed, approach the dead man, speak with him, and ask if he wishes to receive baptism; then when he makes no answer the man who is hidden underneath says instead of him that he wishes to be baptized, and so they baptize him instead of the departed!" Paul would hardly have approved of such a rite!

7. Exodus 23:16, 19

8. Leviticus 23:10, 17

9. This idea is developed in some detail by Aubrey Johnson, *The One and the Many in the Israelite Conception of God* (Cardiff: University of Wales Press Board, 1942). It can be illustrated in Joshua 7:1-26 the story of Achan, who stole some articles from Jericho which had been "devoted to destruction." For that act of disobedience, not only was Achan executed, but also his sons and daughters, cattle, donkeys and sheep, tent and all that he had. The "many" (his whole family) were encompassed in the "one" (Achan).

10. Compare Paul's words in Romans 5:12—"Therefore, just as sin entered the world through one man, and death through sin, and in this way death came to all men, because all sinned" (aorist tense, pointing to one action in the past; i.e., all sinned in Adam.) And 5:15—"But the gift is not like the trespass. For if the many died by the trespass of the one man, how much more did God's grace and the gift that came by the grace of the one man, Jesus Christ, overflow to the many!" This in no way alters the truth that each sinner is accountable to God for his or her own sin. Or that each believer receives the gift of eternal life through his or her own personal faith in Christ.

11. It should be said that verse 22 in no way endorses the idea of universalism.

12. The word translated "turn" is the Greek *tagma*, which originally meant a body of troops. Barrett, p. 354, observes that "in later Greek its use widened, so that it could be applied to any sort of group, military or civilian, and could mean place, or position or even ordinance."

13. 1 Thessalonians 4:16-17

14. For the entire hymn, see *Hymns of the Christian Life*, number 124.

15. Colossians 3:4

16. 1 John 3:1ff

CHAPTER 22

Defining the Resurrection Hope

1 Corinthians 15:35-58

But someone may ask, "How are the dead raised? With what kind of body will they come?" How foolish! What you sow does not come to life unless it dies. When you sow, you do not plant the body that will be, but just a seed, perhaps of wheat or of something else. But God gives it a body as he has determined, and to each kind of seed he gives its own body. All flesh is not the same: Men have one kind of flesh, animals have another, birds another and fish another. There are also heavenly bodies and there are earthly bodies; but the splendor of the heavenly bodies is one kind, and the splendor of the earthly bodies is another. The sun has one kind of splendor, the moon another and the stars another; and star differs from star in splendor.

So will it be with the resurrection of the dead. The body that is sown is perishable, it is raised imperishable; it is sown in dishonor, it is raised in glory; it is sown in weakness, it is raised in power; it is sown a natural body, it is raised a spiritual body.

If there is a natural body, there is also a spiritual body. So it is written: "The first man Adam became a living being"; the last Adam, a life-giving spirit. The spiritual did not come first, but the natural, and after that the spiritual. The first man was of the dust of the earth, the second man

231

*from heaven. As was the earthly man, so are those who are
of the earth; and as is the man from heaven, so also are those
who are of heaven. And just as we have borne the likeness of
the earthly man, so shall we bear the likeness of the man
from heaven.*

*I declare to you, brothers, that flesh and blood cannot
inherit the kingdom of God, nor does the perishable inherit
the imperishable. Listen, I tell you a mystery: We will not
all sleep, but we will all be changed—in a flash, in the
twinkling of an eye, at the last trumpet. For the trumpet
will sound, the dead will be raised imperishable, and we will
be changed. For the perishable must clothe itself with the
imperishable, and the mortal with immortality. When the
perishable has been clothed with the imperishable, and the
mortal with immortality, then the saying that is written
will come true: "Death has been swallowed up in victory."*

> *"Where, O death, is your victory?*
> *Where, O death, is your sting?"*

*The sting of death is sin, and the power of sin is the law. But
thanks be to God! He gives us the victory through our Lord
Jesus Christ.*

*Therefore, my dear brothers, stand firm. Let nothing
move you. Always give yourselves fully to the work of the
Lord, because you know that your labor in the Lord is not
in vain.*

The question was bound to be asked by a skeptical
mind in the Corinthian church, "What kind of a
body is a resurrection body?" How in the world
can dead men possibly rise when their bodies have decayed?
(15:35). Paul sees these objections coming and proceeds to
answer his "foolish" (15:36) questioner.

Some Kinds of Bodies (15:35-41)

He begins by drawing analogies from nature. Even the

Corinthian questioner would know, if he thought about it, that the seed he sows in his garden is not like the plant that will eventually spring up (15:36).[1]

My wife and I live near some enchanting botanical gardens where all summer long acres and acres of gorgeous flowers bloom. In the spring thousands of tulips and daffodils attract visitors from all around North America. To obtain such a dazzling array of beauty, some unattractive bulbs first had to be placed in the ground. The bulb that was sown was not at all like the beautiful flower that emerged. The analogy to human death and resurrection is obvious.

Or take the matter of flesh (15:39). Using a physiology familiar to Judaism,[2] Paul is emphasizing the great variety of differing bodies that exist in the world. There is a wide difference between the flesh of a man, a moose, a magpie or a mackerel. There is also a visible difference (15:40) between earthly bodies (men, animals, birds, fish) and heavenly bodies (sun, moon, stars). And even the heavenly bodies are different one from the other in their brightness (15:41). Paul is saying that, considering the wisdom and power of God that is displayed in the creation of such a variety of objects and creatures, it should not be difficult to envision His ability to create one more thing of intricate beauty—a resurrection body.

An Imperishable Body (15:42-44a)

Referring again to the analogy of sowing and reaping, the apostle makes his point—"So it will be with the resurrection of the dead" (15:42). The lifeless human body that is sown (buried) is described first as perishable (corruptible). Though it does not seem like it, from the moment we are born we begin the process of corruption.

When my wife and I were in China, we viewed the body of Mao Tse-Tung preserved in a vacuum under glass for all to see. We were told to take off our hats and be silent as we passed by all that was left of the Chinese communist leader. I couldn't help thinking of what would happen if the glass that covered his embalmed body were to be shattered. His form would have instantly crumbled into dust and bone. Like all of us, and despite his prominence, Mao possessed a perishable body. In contrast, the body that is raised (resurrected) is described as imperishable (15:42). It will never bear the marks of aging; it will never wrinkle; it will never die. Though recognizable to all who knew it before, it will nevertheless be totally different from what it was.

The body that is "sown" is also described as "sown in dishonor" (15:43a). Leon Morris observes that the word *atimia*, translated "dishonor," was sometimes used of the loss of the rights of citizenship. Says Morris, "A corpse has no rights."[3] The word also means "disgrace," "shameful treatment" or "humiliation"[4]—words that could describe, for example, "indignities cast upon (the body after death) by the living";[5] or our bodies present "lowly bodies" so unlike Christ's glorious body.[6]

In contrast, the resurrected body is said to be "raised in glory." When the disciples were with Jesus on the Mount of Transfiguration, we are told that His face shone like the sun, and His clothes became as white as the light.[7] Alluding to this occasion, the Apostle John later wrote, "We have seen his glory."[8] And Peter recorded, ". . . we were eyewitness of his majesty."[9] The disciples had seen Christ's glory. And in that moment when we are raised from the dead, our new bodies will share that same glory. This is what Paul means when he says that "When Christ, who is [our] life, appears, then you also will appear with him in glory."[10]

Third, the body that dies is said to be "sown in weakness" (15:43b). We see this weakness early, in the defenselessness of childhood. Later we see it in the many infirmities of life—disease, pain and suffering. Finally we see it in the total collapse of all vitality in death. The most cultivated body that a strenuous daily workout can produce has no strength at all compared to the energy that will be inherent in our resurrected body. The body that is laid in the grave is helpless. But in contrast to weakness, Paul says our new bodies will be raised in power. They will be perfectly healthy, fully developed and exempt from the restrictive laws of matter. As an elderly Roman Catholic priest once said to me in describing the power of his glorified body, "It will be able to go through the universe at the speed of light!"

A Heavenly Body (15:44b-49)

Paul now takes up in more detail his fourth comparison between what is sown and what is raised. It is the contrast between the natural (*psuchikon*) body and the spiritual (*pneumatikon*) body (15:44b); that is, between the body of the first man, Adam, and that of the second (last) man, Christ (15:45). Notice how he describes this first man who was created by God and placed in the Garden of Eden: He is said to be "a living being" (15:45); "of the dust of the earth" (15:47); and "earthly" (15:48).[11] The biblical creation account tells us that "the LORD God formed the man from the dust of the ground and breathed into his nostrils the breath of life, and the man became a living being."[12] This was man as he was created to live on earth, a human being able to think, reason and communicate—a natural man, the progenitor of all who are born into the world (15:48a).

Paul contrasts this earthly first man, Adam, with the spiritual second man, Christ. He is described as a life-giving spirit—the One, who by the power inherent in the resurrection, is the source of all spiritual life; the Life imparted to those who are born of the Spirit; and the Life that will be fully manifested in their resurrected bodies. This second Adam is also described as the "man from heaven"—not created from the dust of the earth, but conceived by the Spirit in the womb of a virgin.

Paul is simply telling the Corinthians that the body they now possess—that will eventually die and be buried (sown)—is their inheritance from Adam (15:48a). In contrast, the body that will be resurrected and that will never die again is theirs because of their relationship to Christ (15:48b)—a body just like His resurrected body. "Just as we have borne the likeness of the earthly man, so shall we bear the likeness of the man from heaven" (15:49).

A Death-Defying Body (15:50-58)

How often as a pastor I have stood with a grieving family as the body of their loved one was being lowered into the grave! I have seen their scalding tears and the terrible wrenching away from a husband, a wife, a grandparent, a child. I have seen too the hopeless grief of unbelievers and the tempered sorrow of Christians as the words of the Apostle Paul in this last magnificent section of our text brought comfort and consolation to troubled hearts.

Paul begins by asserting that a new resurrection body is absolutely necessary if anyone would participate in the kingdom of God (15:50). Then he tells his readers how this transformation from flesh and blood to a their new bodies will come about. The nature of the event has been revealed to him by God Himself (15:51).[13] The change, signaled by the trumpet,[14] will happen instantaneously, in the time it takes to flutter an eyelid (15:52). In that moment, those asleep and those still living will be clothed with imperishable, immortal bodies (15:53).

Writing to the Thessalonians, Paul puts the same glorious truth this way:

Brothers, we do not want you to be ignorant about those who fall asleep, or to grieve like the rest of men, who have no hope. We believe that Jesus died and rose again, and so we believe that God will bring with Jesus those who have fallen asleep in him. According to the Lord's own word, we tell you that we who are still alive, who are left till the coming of the Lord, will certainly not precede those who have fallen asleep. For the Lord himself will come down from heaven, with a loud command, with the voice of the archangel and with the trumpet call of God, and the dead in Christ will rise first. After that, we who are still alive and are left will be caught up together with them in the clouds to meet the Lord in the air. And so we will be with the Lord forever. Therefore encourage each other with these words.[15]

This momentous event will mark the victorious destruction of death. Paul draws on his knowledge of the prophets to put his triumphant assertions in biblical language (15:55).[16] In that Day, death will be robbed of its victory and cheated of its sting.[17] But that day has not yet arrived. Death is the last enemy to be destroyed (15:26), and the moment for its defeat has not yet come. It is sin, strengthened by the law,[18] that puts the dread in death (15:56). But Christ has "redeemed us from the curse of the law, being made a curse for us."[19] By His atoning death, He has dealt thoroughly with the problem of sin, and believers in Him need not fear death. In this knowledge and hope, they are exhorted to stand firm in their faith, giving themselves fully to the work of the Lord because "[they] know that [their] labor in the Lord is not in vain" (15:58).

Conclusion

Paul has thoroughly answered the questions of the Corinthian skeptic, "How are the dead raised? With what kind of body will they come?" Using analogies from the natural world, he has shown that it is perfectly reasonable to believe that God could and would create resurrection bodies for believers.

He has shown that these resurrection bodies are identical to the resurrection body of our risen Lord Jesus Christ and that they are necessary if we would participate in the kingdom of God. Furthermore, the transformation from a perishable to an imperishable body will take place in a flash at the glorious appearing of our God and Savior, and in that moment death will be "swallowed up in victory."

What a blessed hope we believers possess![20] We are assured of it because we have been marked (sealed) as God's own, through the indwelling of the Holy Spirit.[21] His in-dwelling is the "deposit guaranteeing our inheritance until the redemption of those who are God's possession."[22] We are taught that "if the Spirit of him who raised Jesus from the dead is living in [us], he who raised Christ from the dead will also give live to [our] mortal bodies through his Spirit, who lives in [us].[23]

We can sing with joy one other stanza of Charles Wesley's great Easter hymn:

> Lives again our glorious King; Alleluia!
> Where, O death, is now thy sting? Alleluia!
> Dying once, He all doth save: Alleluia!
> Where's thy victory, O grave? Alleluia!

Endnotes

1. The emphasis in the phrase, "What you sow . . ." (15:36) is on the word "you"—(*su ho speireis*), as though Paul were saying, "Even *you* have had enough experience to know this."

2. See Barrett, 371.

3. p. 227.

4. See Arndt and Gingrich, 119.

5. See Edwards, 439.

6. Philippians 3:21

7. Matthew 17:2

8. John 1:14

9. 2 Peter 1:16

10. Colossians 3:4

11. The word is *choikos*—made of dust.

12. Genesis 2:7. The Hebrew translated "living being" is *nephesh chayah* ("living soul"). Man is said to have *become* a soul.

13. The word "mystery" in the New Testament refers to information that could not have been known unless God had revealed it. And He has revealed it.

14. The sounding of a trumpet in the Old Testament marks such events as the year of jubilee (Leviticus 25:9), a call to arms (Judges 6:34), the coronation of a king (1 Kings 1:34), the calling of captives home from captivity (Isaiah 27:13) and most importantly for our text, the signaling of the Day of the Lord (Joel 2:1; Zechariah 9:14).

15. 1 Thessalonians 4:13-18

16. He uses Isaiah 25:8 and Hosea 13:14 loosely quoted.

17. "The word *kentron* refers to the sting of bees, serpents and the like. This metaphorical use pictures the harmfulness of death. It is a malignant adversary." See Morris, 234.

18. See Romans 7:7ff, for the relationship between sin and the law.

19. Galatians 3:13

20. Titus 2:13

21. The Holy Spirit Himself is the mark.

22. Ephesians 1:14

23. Romans 8:11

CHAPTER 23

Enjoining Wise Stewardship

1 Corinthians 16

Now about the collection for God's people: Do what I told the Galatian churches to do. On the first day of every week, each one of you should set aside a sum of money in keeping with his income, saving it up, so that when I come no collections will have to be made. Then, when I arrive, I will give letters of introduction to the men you approve and send them with your gift to Jerusalem. If it seems advisable for me to go also, they will accompany me.

After I go through Macedonia, I will come to you—for I will be going through Macedonia. Perhaps I will stay with you awhile, or even spend the winter, so that you can help me on my journey, wherever I go. I do not want to see you now and make only a passing visit; I hope to spend some time with you, if the Lord permits. But I will stay on at Ephesus until Pentecost, because a great door for effective work has opened to me, and there are many who oppose me.

If Timothy comes, see to it that he has nothing to fear while he is with you, for he is carrying on the work of the Lord, just as I am. No one, then, should refuse to accept him. Send him on his way in peace so that he may return to me. I am expecting him along with the brothers.

Now about our brother Apollos: I strongly urged him to go to you with the brothers. He was quite unwilling to go now, but he will go when he has the opportunity.

Be on your guard; stand firm in the faith; be men of courage; be strong. Do everything in love.

You know that the household of Stephanas were the first converts in Achaia, and they have devoted themselves to the service of the saints. I urge you, brothers, to submit to such as these and to everyone who joins in the work, and labors at it. I was glad when Stephanas, Fortunatus and Achaicus arrived, because they have supplied what was lacking from you. For they refreshed my spirit and yours also. Such men deserve recognition.

The churches in the province of Asia send you greetings. Aquila and Priscilla greet you warmly in the Lord, and so does the church that meets at their house. All the brothers here send you greetings. Greet one another with a holy kiss.

I, Paul, write this greeting in my own hand.

If anyone does not love the Lord—a curse be on him. Come, O Lord!

The grace of the Lord Jesus be with you.

My love to all of you in Christ Jesus. Amen.

We are reaching the end of Paul's apostolic letter called First Corinthians. It must have taken him considerable time to write this letter which covered many different subjects and required him to deal with themes that would make him even less popular with some church members than he already was. While he wrote it, he was engaged in intense evangelistic and pastoral ministries in Ephesus and was probably earning his living making tents as well.

One subject dear to his heart still must be addressed, and he would like to express personal concerns before final words of greeting are delivered.

A Stewardship of Money (16:1-4)

Giving aid to the poor, the needy and the destitute has always been close to the heart of Christian people. In most local churches, benevolent funds assist needy individuals who have experienced a financial emergency. When we hear about catastrophes at home or abroad, our hearts go out to the victims, and we immediately receive offerings to relieve our brothers and sisters in distress. So it was also in Paul's day. The Christians in Jerusalem were in need of financial assistance, and other churches sprang into action.

We do not know the reason for the collection to which our text refers (16:1). During the reign of the Roman emperor Claudius (A.D. 41-54), a famine predicted by the Jerusalem prophet Agabus had brought the Christians of Judea into severe straits. The church at Antioch in Syria had decided to send financial aid by Barnabas and Paul.[1] It seems unlikely, however, that this was the collection to which Paul is referring.

We know the church in Jerusalem was comparatively poor. The city of Jerusalem was not rich, depending largely on the generosity of Jews from outside Palestine. Poor Christians, who were the objects of persecution from their fellow Jews,[2] would hardly receive any of this help, and could only look to other Christians for aid. The leaders of the Jerusalem church had asked Paul to remember the poor, and Paul, who felt a moral obligation to them,[3] had expressed eagerness to comply with their request.[4]

Evidently he had presented the need to the church at Corinth, and they, along with the Macedonian churches, had been among the first to express a willingness to help.[5] In response to their request about how they should collect the money,[6] Paul gives the same instructions he had given the Galatian churches.[7]

First, the benevolent money was to be set aside "[o]n the first day of every week" (16:2). This gives some evidence about the day Christians worshiped together. Our Lord Jesus was raised from the dead on the first day of the week, and the disciples chose to commemorate this momentous event on "the Lord's Day," distinct from the Jewish Sabbath. It seems likely Paul is instructing the Corinthians to bring their gifts to the church treasury when they come together on Sunday to worship.

Second, "each one of you" (16:2) without regard for their financial condition was to take the opportunity to participate in the offering. Paul marveled at the way the Macedonian churches had responded to his appeal. He attributes their generosity to the manifestation of God's grace that enabled them to give beyond their ability. "Out of the most severe trial, their overflowing joy and their extreme poverty welled up in rich generosity."[8] So with the Corinthians, the less affluent were not to exclude themselves from the blessing accorded generosity. Paul would tell them that "[w]hoever sows sparingly will also reap sparingly, and whoever sows generously will also reap generously."[9]

Third, each should give "a sum of money in keeping with his income" (16:2). Paul indicates no set amount or proportion of income to be given, but leaves that to each person's conscience or the guidance of the Holy Spirit. In his second letter to them, Paul says, "Each man should give what he has decided in his heart to give, not reluctantly or under compulsion, for God loves a cheerful giver."[10]

The Old Covenant practice of tithing assured that each person would give the same proportion to the Lord. This has been the custom of many of God's people through the years and has been a habit that God has genuinely blessed. Paul never mentions it, preferring rather to leave the proportion to their own prayerful choice.

Fourth, the purpose for this procedure is "that when I come no collections will have to be made" (16:2). If Paul was not comfortable taking up offerings, he would surely be uncomfortable with some of today's methods to extract funds. Or perhaps he felt other things should better occupy his time and effort. Or maybe he just did not wish to touch the money. Judging from what he says next, it was probably the latter.

Paul takes meticulous care in the handling of this offering. "I will give letters of introduction to the men you approve and send them with your gift to Jerusalem" (16:3).[11] He wants to give the Corinthians no occasion to accuse him of misappropriation of funds. One can only pray that today's church "fund-raisers" would exercise the same scrupulous care.

When I became pastor of one assembly, the church treasurer counted the Sunday offerings by himself behind a closed door. When I casually suggested he should have some help, he retorted, "What's the matter, don't you trust me?" His reply made me think that perhaps I shouldn't. I explained that by counting the money alone, he was leaving himself open to possible allegations of dishonesty.

Just what Paul means in 16:4 by "[i]f it seems advisable for me to go also, they will accompany me" is not clear. Perhaps his going depended on the size of the offering received. Perhaps there were other considerations.[12] He did, in fact, end up going.[13]

A Stewardship of Time (16:5-9)

Paul now takes up some matters having to do with his own plans, and with his concerns for some of his coworkers. First, our text indicates his plans to visit the Corinthians were uncertain. He anticipated traveling from Ephesus to Macedonia and then possibly to Corinth to "stay . . . a while, or even spend the winter" (16:5-6).[14] He would, however, "stay on at Ephesus until Pentecost" (16:8) because "a great door for effective work has opened [literally 'stands open'] to me, and there are many who oppose me" (16:9).

Paul was always conscious of opportunities to evangelize, and Ephesus had presented one such great opportunity. Luke's record in Acts 19 tells us that "Paul entered the synagogue and spoke boldly there for three months, arguing persuasively about the kingdom of God." When he was forced to preach elsewhere, he "had discussions daily in the lecture hall of Tyrannus" for two years, "so that all the Jews and Greeks who lived in the province of Asia heard the word of the Lord." The great number of public confessions of faith and burning of sorcery scrolls caused the "word of the Lord [to] spread widely and [grow] in power."

But with increased opportunity comes increased opposition. My pastor-father used to say, "Whenever God is blessing, we can expect to see the devil angry!" So it was in Ephesus where some "refused to believe and publicly maligned the Way."[15] One of the most prominent opposers of Paul's message was the silversmith Demetrius, who feared the growing number of Christians would depress the idol market. He stirred up a riot in the city that appeared to endanger Paul's life, which was only quieted by the intervention of the city clerk. After this, Paul encouraged the disciples and left for Macedonia.[16]

A Stewardship of Courtesy (1 Corinthians 16:10-18)

Paul now presents the names of several Christian workers to whom he wants the Corinthians to show consideration and respect. First is Timothy, his youthful son in the faith.[17] In 4:17, Paul had expressed his intention to send his assistant ("my son whom I love") to act on his behalf. Now recognizing that some in Corinth might make things unpleasant for Timothy, he urges the church to do nothing that might frighten him, but rather to accept him and "[s]end him on his way in peace" (16:10-11).

Second, he mentions Apollos, whom the Corinthians had evidently mentioned in their letter to Paul, apparently requesting that he visit them again.[18] Paul, who does not see Apollos as a rival, is agreeable to their desire and "strongly urged him to go to [them] with the brothers" (16:12). Paul was not one to be jealous of another's God-given gifts and would have thanked God for this mighty Alexandrian teacher of the Word who held such a high place in the hearts of some Corinthian believers. His only concern would be that those who loved Apollos' ministry not create division in the church.[19] Apollos, however, was not prepared to go back to Corinth at this time (16:12b).

A Stewardship of Courage (16:13-14)

Before he mentions other colleagues, Paul expresses a final concern for the church. He gives the Corinthians five succinct exhortations, which are not immediately connected with what precedes or follows. It seems the condition of the Corinthian church suddenly comes to his mind—"a state of spiritual lethargy, vacillation, childish weakness and selfishness"[20]—and he must show them a better way.

1. "Be on your guard," he writes. The word is simply "watch" or "stay awake" and is used in the New Testament for both moral vigilance and looking out for the return of Christ.

2. "[S]tand firm in the faith." Paul desires that their trust in God and obedience to Him be unswerving. Many had manifested traits of instability that concerned the apostle.

3. "[B]e men of courage." They were up against an adversary bent on destroying their faith and the church. They must recognize the true nature of their foe and bravely stand against him.

4. "[B]e strong." The Greek verb may be translated "be made strong," indicating that the source of their strength was not in themselves, but in God, their Strength. In these last two exhortations, Paul may have had in mind the words of the Lord to Joshua, on the verge of entering the land of Canaan—"Be strong and very courageous. Be careful to obey all the law my servant Moses gave you."[21]

5. "Do everything in love." He had set before them in chapter 13 the preeminence, practice and permanence of love. He reminds them here that their entire lives should be lived in such an atmosphere.

A Stewardship of Submission (16:15-18)

Paul now returns to expressing his concern for colleagues. Not only Timothy and Apollos were on his heart, but the family of Stephanas. They "were the first converts in Achaia" and had appointed themselves[22] in a spirit of humility "to the service of the saints" (16:15). They had seen a need and filled it without any official appointment. Paul recognized the legitimacy of their ministry and urged submission on the part of the church to them[23] and to all who join in the work (16:16).

Two others besides Stephanas—Fortunatus and Achaicus—had "refreshed" Paul's spirit by their presence (16:17-18). The apostle was likely missing his friends in Corinth, and these three brethren made up for that lack. They therefore deserve recognition by their home church. Paul was an affirmer of faithful Christian workers, whatever their ministry.

A Stewardship of Grace (16:19-24)

As one might expect, Paul's letter concludes with greetings from individuals and churches with which the Corinthians were familiar. The churches in Asia, Aquila and Priscilla and their house-church and the Ephesian believers all send their regards. As was his custom, Paul, who had dictated his letter, adds his closing greetings in his own handwriting.

Paul's feeling that love for the Lord is the mark of a true Christian[24] is so deep that he pronounces a curse on anyone who does not have it (16:22). The words translated "Come, O Lord" are from an Aramaic expression "Maranatha," expressing a sentiment extremely important to the members of the early Church. It reminds us of the prayer in Revelation 22:20 KJV, "Even so, come, Lord Jesus," depicting the eager longing felt by the Church for the speedy return of the Lord.

Paul pronounces his oft-repeated blessing on the church— "The grace of the Lord Jesus be with you"—and sends his love to all who are in Christ Jesus (1 Corinthians 16:23-24).

Conclusion

There is much we can learn and apply to our lives from this concluding chapter of Paul's letter to the Corinthians. First, our text reminds us of the importance of systematic, proportionate, generous giving to the work of the Lord, whether on behalf of the poor or the ministry of the Church in general. It is true that "God loves a cheerful giver."[25]

Second, it is important to be what one of my former professors called "witness conscious." As Paul recognized and entered open doors of evangelism, so we must be alert to opportunities that come to us in the providence of God to bear witness to Christ and His saving power. At the same time, we must not be discouraged when the enemy comes in like a flood with his temptations to discouragement or defeatism. It is not unlike our enemy to suggest that we are not worthy to share our faith. As Peter put it to his readers, "Your enemy the devil prowls around like a roaring lion looking for someone to devour. Resist him."[26]

Finally I must repeat the importance of reverent submission to the Word of God as it is proclaimed by his servants and humble submission one to another in the Body of Christ. Submission to another is not instinctive to the natural man, yet is one of the marks of the Spirit-filled life (Ephesians 5:21).

Endnotes

1. Acts 11:27-30

2. See 1 Thessalonians 2:14ff

3. See Romans 15:25-27

4. Galatians 2:9-10

5. See 2 Corinthians 8 and 9. By the time Paul wrote Second Corinthians, it seems that the Corinthian church had faltered somewhat in completing the collection they had begun to receive. In this second letter, the apostle goes into great detail concerning the importance of generous giving, urging the church to finish the job it had started.

6. He begins chapter 16 with the same formula used in chapters 7, 8 and 12—"Now about" (*peri de*). Chapter 7

begins with, "Now for the matters you wrote about," indicating that he was replying to questions they had raised in a letter to him.

7. Though the Corinthians had likely heard of them, we have no record of the instructions Paul had given to the churches of Galatia in this matter.

8. 2 Corinthians 8:2ff

9. 2 Corinthians 9:6

10. 2 Corinthians 9:7

11. Morris, p. 239, states, "Such letters of commendation were common, and Deissmann [Light from the Ancient Past] cites one dated 12th September, A.D. 50."

12. Morris, p. 239, states, "It would not be seemly for an apostle to supervise in person the delivery of a niggardly amount." Moffatt, p. 270, freely translates, "If the sum makes it worth my while to go too, they shall accompany me." On the other hand, Edwards, p. 466, thinks that Paul hesitated to go himself "from a sense of delicacy and fear of being obtrusive, and not from any notion that it would be unworthy of an Apostle to carry a small sum."

13. See Romans 15:25 and Acts 21:16

14. It seems that for some reason, his plans were postponed. He writes in Second Corinthians 1:16, "I planned to visit you on my way to Macedonia and to come back to you from Macedonia, and then to have you send me on my way to Judea. When I planned this, did I do it lightly?" The implied answer is, "No." Then in verse 23, he explains, "I call God as my witness that it was in order to spare you that I did not return to Corinth. . . . So I made up my mind that I would not make another painful visit to you." He evidently wants to give them time to carry out his directives given in the first letter.

15. Acts 19:9. Followers of Jesus, were said to be followers of "the Way"—the Jesus Way.

16. The whole story is told in Acts 19:23-20:1.

17. 1 Timothy 1:2

18. Verse 12 begins with the now familiar formula, "now about," indicating that they had mentioned Apollos in their letter to Paul.

19. See again chapter 1 of the letter.

20. Edwards, 470.

21. Joshua 1:7

22. The verb translated in the NIV as "devoted" (*etaksan*) could more properly be translated, "appointed." See Arndt and Gingrich, p. 813. The word does not so much denote earnestness, as a voluntary setting themselves apart to the work. Moffat, p. 278, states that this word is "a trade metaphor which Plato happens to use . . . about tradesmen who 'set themselves to the business of serving the public,' by retailing farm produce, since they 'saw the need of this.' "

23. The verb in 16:16, "to submit" is *hupotasso*; the verb in 16:15, "appoint" is *tasso*. It appears that Paul is making a play on words.

24. It is interesting to notice that the verb "to love" which he uses here is *phileo* rather than the usual *agapao*. This is the only place in his writings where he uses this verb, and this may indicate, as Barrett observes, p. 396, that he is quoting a current Christian formula.

25. 2 Corinthians 9:7

26. 1 Peter 5:8-9

First Corinthians and the Deeper Life

This volume is part of the series entitled *The Deeper Life Pulpit Commentary*. The purpose of the series is to present from the entire Scriptures the challenge of the deeper life. Before we attempt to summarize the part that First Corinthians plays in drawing us into a deeper life with God, we need to first be sure we understand the meaning of the expression, "deeper life."

What Is "the Deeper Life"?

In a real sense, we can say that the deeper Christian life is the *normal* Christian life. Our Alliance Statement of Faith presents it in these words:

> It is the will of God that each believer should be filled with the Holy Spirit and be sanctified wholly, being separated from sin and the world and fully dedicated to the will of God, thereby receiving power for holy living and effective service. This is both a crisis and a progressive experience wrought in the life of the believer subsequent to conversion.

Notice that the deeper life is a life devoted to Holy Spirit-enabled holy living. I would define this as growth in Christlikeness. To live such a life necessitates, as the statement declares, that we be "filled with the Spirit" (Ephesians 5:18), an experience that is recognized as both a post-conversion crisis and an ongoing process in the believer's life. Furthermore, living a holy life involves our putting off the "works of the flesh" by the power of the Holy Spirit (Galatians 5:19-20; Romans 8:12-13) and allowing the disposition of Christ (the "fruit of the Spirit") to grow in us, as we yield to Him (Galatians 5:22-23).

Second, we observe that the deeper Christian life is one that is empowered by the Holy Spirit for ministry. Christ promised this enablement to His disciples just before He ascended to His Father (Acts 1:8). This same enduement of power is available to the Church today and is an absolute "must" if we are to carry out our Lord's mandate to evangelize the world. It is, furthermore, a life that is commanded of believers in the Scripture (Ephesians 5:18; Luke 24:49).

How may we enter into the "deeper Christian life?" While each believer will have an individual pilgrimage with God in this important matter, certain principles are common to all.

1. We must recognize that being filled with the Spirit is a valid experience for believers that each may have.

2. There will need to be a deep heart hunger for the fullness of the Spirit (Matthew 5:6).

3. Repentance, a turning away from whatever we know to be displeasing to God, is a prerequisite for being filled.

4. We must ask the risen Christ to fill us (Luke 11:13).

5. There must come a definite crisis moment in our praying in which we surrender ourselves unconditionally to the full Lordship of Christ and by faith invite the Holy Spirit to come and fill our lives.

The deeper life is maintained by continued obedience to the will of God, confessing our sins whenever necessary and receiving God's forgiveness (1 John 1:9); by a continual attitude of praise and thanksgiving (Ephesians 5:18ff); through meditation in the Word of God and devotion to prayer; and through faithful service to Christ and His Church according to our giftedness.

The Contribution of First Corinthians

First Corinthians calls believers to be united around the Person and work of our Lord Jesus Christ. It is to Him, not Paul, Apollos or Peter or their modern counterparts (these men are God's fellow workers), that we owe our ultimate loyalty. Human wisdom would tend to make us human-centered rather than Christ-centered and draw us away from the true wisdom of God—found in the cross. We need to be careful to maintain the "unity of the Spirit, in the bond of peace" (chapters 1-3).

While we do not exalt our spiritual leaders, at the same time, we who aspire to Christlikeness must be careful not to stand in judgment on them. It is incumbent upon them to be faithful to their calling; it is incumbent upon us to respect and honor them as servants of God and to give heed to the Word they preach. Nothing is more destructive of healthy church life than a destructively critical tongue. We must take heed to our Lord's command, "Do not judge, or you too will be judged" (chapter 4).

In all our proper concern for the numerical growth of our churches, we must be just as concerned for the moral purity of the assembly. When we remember that our bodies are the temples of the Holy Spirit, sexual immorality can never be made compatible with a holy life. Sin is the exception in a believer's life, not the rule (chapters 5-6).

As "deeper life" Christians, one of our concerns has got to be for the reputation of Christ and His Church among unbelievers. Rather than bring our disputes before the world and besmirch our Savior's name, we ought rather to settle them within the boundaries of the church or else allow ourselves to be wronged (chapter 6).

In these days when almost half of all marriages end in divorce, our letter calls upon believers to hold the God-ordained institution of marriage in high regard. Husbands and wives manifest their love by living unselfishly for each other's good. Divorce is not an option for those who are walking in the Spirit. Although it is not always easy to do so, believers dedicated to doing the will of God will need to discover how to properly balance their responsibilities to God, to His Church, to their families and to themselves (chapter 7).

One of the most important lessons from First Corinthians is the importance of considering the spiritual well-being of our fellow believers. Our personal consciences may allow us to engage in morally neutral practices, but if it becomes evident that our behavior would cause a "weaker" brother or sister to be offended or fall away from their faith, then for love's sake we must refrain from doing what otherwise we would be free to do (chapters 8-9). But we must also be careful that we stay as far away as possible from whatever would decrease our love for God, lest like Israel of old we allow ourselves to be drawn into outright sin (chapter 10).

The spirit of the age is bent upon destroying the God-ordained, biblical distinctions in the roles of men and women. First Corinthians calls us to recognize the spiritual oneness of Christian men and women, and at the same time recognize that our roles are indeed different. The "headship" of the man and the voluntary submission of the woman mirrors the relationship between the Father and the Son. As those who aspire to holiness of life, our public behavior, especially within the Church, should manifest our willingness to accept this biblical pattern (chapter 11).

The ministry of the Holy Spirit in gifting the members of Christ's body is given for the building up of the Church. It is the prerogative of the Spirit to dispense His diverse gifts and the manifestations of His love and power as He sees fit. No gift is without significance and usefulness in the body. Nor is any one ministry independent of other ministries (chapter 12). All supernatural ministry within the Church must be calculated to encourage, strengthen and comfort the mem-

bers. Gifts of the Spirit should not exercised in self-aggran-
dizing ways or in ways that disrupt the peace and order of
the assembly (chapter 14).

All gifts, manifestations and ministries are to be governed
by a spirit of Christian love. Be they ever so spectacular,
gifts that are exercised in unloving ways are not profitable
either for the one who exercises them or for the rest of the
Church. The kind of love that we are called to as believers,
seeks, wherever possible, to unselfishly meet the real needs
of others. This kind of love will never fail (chapter 13).

Central to the entire Christian faith is the monumental
historical fact of the bodily resurrection of Jesus Christ. He
died for our sins, was buried and was raised on the third day
by the power of God. His resurrection was validated by
more than 500 witnesses. The resurrection of Jesus assures
the resurrection from the dead of all who believe on Him.
Until that great Day when He comes to be glorified in His
people, Christ calls us to stand firm in our faith, giving ourselves fully to the work of the Lord (chapter 15).

The Word of God calls us to be good stewards of His
money. Whether helping the poor or supporting the work of
the Church at home or abroad, each believer is called to give
gladly as God has prospered him. Those responsible for the
management of these funds are to be men of unsullied integrity (chapter 16).

One principle that runs throughout this letter is that of
submission one to another—submission of the Son to the
Father; the submission of all to the Lord Jesus; of wives to
husbands; of members to godly leadership; of "strong" to
"weak"; of "weak" to "strong"; each to the other. In his
Ephesian letter, Paul tells us that we keep on being filled
with the Spirit, through praise, thanksgiving and mutual
submission.

It was the "fleshly" refusal to walk in humble and loving
submission to each other that created the great majority of the
Corinthian church's problems. The spirit of the world—"me
first," "my rights," "my way"—had invaded this assembly of

the saints and is always ready to encroach on our churches today. We need to guard against this manifestation of the flesh.

Finally, at the heart of the Apostle Paul's instructive and corrective letter was a deep, pure, unconditional love for the Church. Call it "tough love," but his honesty, his stern language and his unbending attachment to principle were but a demonstration of a love that was willing to lay down its life for the glory of God and the good of God's people.

May God enable us who seek to live the deeper Christian life, to apply to our daily Christian walk the lessons that First Corinthians would bring to us.

BIBLIOGRAPHY

Arndt, William F. and Gingrich, F. Wilbur. *A Greek-English Lexicon of the New Testament*. A translation and adaptation of Walter Bauer's German Lexicon. Chicago, IL: The University of Chicago Press, 1957.

Baird, William. *The Corinthian Church—A Biblical Approach to Urban Culture*. Nashville, TN: Abingdon Press, 1946.

Barclay, William. *The Letters to the Corinthians*. Philadelphia, PA: The Westminster Press, 1977.

Barrett, C.K. *A Commentary on the First Epistle to the Corinthians*. London: Adam & Charles Black, 1968.

Baxter, J. Sidlow. *A New Call to Holiness*. Grand Rapids, MI: Zondervan Publishing House, 1973.

Bittlinger, Arnold. *Gifts and Graces*. Translation from German by Herbert Klassen. Grand Rapids, MI: William B. Eerdmans Publishing Company, 1967.

Bristow, John Temple. *What Paul Really Said about Women*. San Francisco, CA: Harper & Row, 1988.

Byrne, Brendan. *Paul and the Christian Woman*. Collegeville, MI: The Liturgical Press, 1988.

Calvin, John. *Commentary on the Epistles of Paul the Apostle to the Corinthians*, vol. I. Edinburgh: The Calvin Translation Society, 1848.

Christenson, Larry. *Speaking in Tongues*. Minneapolis, MN: Dimension Books, 1968.

Delitzsch, F. *Commentary on the Old Testament*, vol. VII, "Isaiah." Grand Rapids, MI: William B. Eerdmans Publishing Company, reprinted in 1975.

Dods, Marcus. *The First Epistle to the Corinthians*. New York, NY: Hodder & Stoughton, n.d.

Edwards, Thomas. *A Commentary on the First Epistle to the Corinthians*. Minneapolis, MN: Klock & Klock Publishers, 1979 reprint from 1885.

Fee, Gordon. *The First Epistle to the Corinthians*. Grand Rapids, MI: William B. Eerdmans Publishing Company, 1987.

Findlay, G.C. "St. Paul's First Epistle to the Corinthians", *The Expositor's Greek Testament*, Vol. 2. Grand Rapids, MI: William B. Eerdmans Publishing Company, n.d.

Glen, J. Stanley. *Pastoral Problems in First Corinthians*. Philadelphia, PA: The Westminster Press, 1964.

Gooch, Peter. *Dangerous Food*. Waterloo, Ontario: Wilfred Laurier University Press, 1993.

Grosheide, F.W. *Commentary on the First Epistle to the Corinthians*. Grand Rapids, MI: William B. Eerdmans Publishing Company, 1976.

Horton, Harold. *The Gifts of the Spirit*. Nottingham: Assemblies of God Publishing House, 1934.

Hurly, James. *Man and Woman in Biblical Perspective*. Grand Rapids, MI: Zondervan Publishing House, 1981.

Keener, Craig S. *Paul, Women and Wives*. Peabody, MA: Hendrickson Publishers, 1992.

Kittel, Gerhard and Friedrich, Gerhard, eds. *Theological Dictionary of the New Testament*. 10 Volumes. Grand Rapids, MI: William B. Eerdmans Publishing Company, 1964

Lloyd-Jones, Martyn. *Studies in the Sermon on the Mount*, vol. I. Grand Rapids, MI: William B. Eerdmans Publishing Company, 1964.

MacArthur, John E. *The Gospel According to Jesus*. Grand Rapids, MI: Zondervan Publishing House, 1988.

Mallone, George. *Those Controversial Gifts*. Downers Grove, IL: InterVarsity Press, 1983.

Marshall, I. Howard. *Kept by the Power of God*. Minneapolis, MN: Bethany Fellowship, Inc., 1969.

Moffatt, James. *The First Epistle of Paul to the Corinthians*. New York, NY: Harper and Brothers Publishers, n.d.

Morris, Leon. *The First Epistle of Paul to the Corinthians*. London: Tyndale Press, 1958.

Orr, James. *The Christian View of God and the World*. Grand Rapids, MI: William B. Eerdmans Publishing Company, 1954.

Pawson, David. *The Normal Christian Birth*. London: Hodder & Stoughton, 1989.

Pearson, Birger A. *The Pneumatikos-Psychicos Terminology in 1 Corinthians*. Missoula, MT: Scholars Press, 1973.

Piper, John & Grudem, Wayne, eds. *Recovering Biblical Manhood and Womanhood*. Wheaton, IL: Crossway Books, 1991

Snyder, Graydon F. *First Corinthians, a Faith Community*. Macon, GA: Mercer University Press, 1992.

Stronstad, Roger. *The Charismatic Theology of St. Luke*. Peabody, MA: Hendrickson Publishers.

Tenney, Merrill C. ed. *The Zondervan Pictorial Bible Dictionary*. Grand Rapids, MI: Zondervan Publishing House, 1967.

_____. *New Testament Survey*. Grand Rapids, MI: William B. Eerdmans Publishing Company, 1961.

Tozer, A.W. *The Pursuit of God*. Harrisburg, PA: Christian Publications, Inc., 1948.

_____. *Tragedy in the Church: The Missing Gifts*. Harrisburg, PA: Christian Publications, Inc., 1978.

Trench, Richard Chenevix. *Synonyms of the New Testament*. Grand Rapids, MI: William B. Eerdmans Publishing Company, 1948.

Wallis, Arthur. *Pray in the Spirit*. London: Victory Press, 1970.

White, John. *When the Spirit Comes with Power*. Downers Grove, IL: Inter-Varsity Press, 1988.